Y0-DWP-300

66 FAMILY HANDYMAN®
WOOD PROJECTS

No. 2632
$21.95

66 FAMILY HANDYMAN®
WOOD PROJECTS

EDITORS OF THE FAMILY HANDYMAN®

TAB BOOKS Inc.
Blue Ridge Summit, PA 17214

FIRST EDITION
FIRST PRINTING

Library of Congress Cataloging in Publication Data
Main entry under title:

66 Family handyman wood projects.

Includes index.
1. Woodwork. 2. Furniture making.
3. Do-it-yourself work. I. Family handyman.
II. Title: Sixty-six Family handyman wood projects.
TT180.A12   1985   684.1′04   85-17319
ISBN 0-8306-0464-2
ISBN 0-8306-1164-9 (pbk.)

Front cover photograph courtesy of The Family Handyman® magazine.

Contents

66 FAMILY HANDYMAN®
WOOD PROJECTS

Also by the Authors from TAB BOOKS, Inc.

No. 1122 *77 Furniture Projects You Can Build*

Introduction

If you enjoy working with wood and working around your house—whether you're a first-time or a seasoned do-it-yourselfer—you'll enjoy this volume by the editors of *The Family Handyman®*. In it you'll find a cornucopia of ideas for every room in the house—as well as your garage and backyard.

Furniture, storage projects, home-improvement ideas—they're all covered here, and you're sure to find projects that will keep you busy for hours building and using them. Some projects are small in the amount of hours they take to construct, but huge in the amount of time and money savings they'll afford you. Other projects will take a considerable amount of time, but they will still be worth every minute you spend on them. All the projects are worth their weight in the enjoyment your family will receive as they work, or play, or relax.

Whatever your needs now or in the future, the ideas presented in this book will be sure to at least start you on the way to meeting those needs. The fun and experience you gain as you build these projects will be an added feature. So pick a subject, buy the materials, look over the instructions and diagrams, and begin your own wood project.

Chapter 1

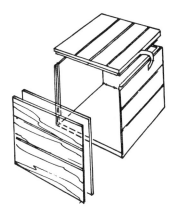

Living Room/
Family Room Projects

You can make your own living room furniture and storage shelves. The projects in this chapter will help you get started, and all of them will look professional. To start, you can make the following mantelpiece for your fireplace. Then you can go on to the bar, storage wall, and other projects given here.

MAKE A BEAUTIFUL MANTELPIECE

An attractive fireplace mantel can do a great deal to improve the appearance of a room. Today there are very good looking mantels made up in kits of precut ponderosa pine parts that are not only easy to assemble but can be adjusted in height and width to fit your fireplace. You can, of course, also make a mantel from scratch, using the list of materials shown in Table 1-1.

In Fig. 1-1, the pilasters (B) are L-shaped at the back. In the kit they appear to be one piece, but actually they are two pieces glued together. If you make your own pilasters you will have to glue the smaller strip (A) to the back of B. The backing strips (C) fit into the offset or rabbet behind the pilasters and are fastened to them from the back with screws.

Like the backing strips, the ends of the frieze (D) fit into the offset behind the pilasters where they are fastened with glue and screws driven from behind the frieze. The tops of the backing strips (C) have tongues which fit into the groove that runs the length of the frieze's bottom edge.

To lower the height of the mantel the backing strip (C) is removed, and the pilasters are cut at the bottom so that they are even with the top of the base block. The backing strip is then restored to its position and now projects beyond the base block. The backing strip is now cut off even with the bottom of the base block.

Shortening the width of the mantel is easily accomplished by removing its top molding (J) and cutting straight through the frieze (D) and its lower molding (K). The top pilaster moldings and the top frieze molding (J) are mitered where they meet. Therefore, after shortening the frieze, this top

1

A.	1 pcs, 3/4″ × 2″ × 52″
B.	2 pcs, 3/4″ × 4″ × 52″
C.	2 pcs, 3/4″ × 4″ × 43 1/2″
D.	1 pc, 3/4″ × 13 1/2″ × 71″
E.	13 ft. of molding
F.	1 pc, 1 3/4″ × 7″ × 83 1/8″
G.	1 pc, 1 3/4″ × 83 1/8″
H.	1 pc, 3/4″ × 5″ × 5″
I.	1 pc, 3/4″ × 2 1/2″ × 5″
J.	1 pc, 1 1/2″ × 2″ × 71″
BB.	9 ft. of molding on frieze and pilasters
GG.	2 pcs, 1 3/4″ × 83 1/8″

Table 1-1. Materials for the Mantelpiece.

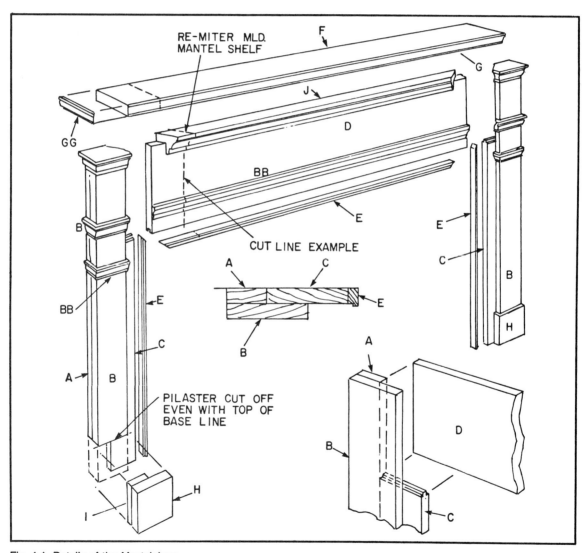

Fig. 1-1. Details of the Mantelpiece.

molding (J) will have to be remitered to make it fit.

The lower molding on the frieze (BB) does not have to be removed or mitered because the pilasters are *coped*, or cut out, at the back to allow it to fit. If the frieze is reduced in width by 4 inches, the shelf (F) and its moldings (G) should be reduced by the same amount. If, however, the frieze has been reduced by 2 inches or less, the top shelf can be left intact since the slight amount of added overhang will not spoil the proportions of the mantel. The shelf is attached to the pilaster tops and the frieze with finishing nails that are set and the holes puttied.

The scribe strips are shortened according to the change in the height of the pilasters and the width of the frieze. These strips are mitered.

With the entire mantel assembled, the last step is to fasten it to the wall. The type of fastener to use depends on what the wall is made of. If it is bricks or masonry, use masonry fasteners; if you can reach wood studs use nails. Gently pry up the lowest molding on the pilasters and remove them. Then drive nails or drill holes for masonry fasteners and apply them. Now restore the moldings to their position.

Remove the base blocks (H) at the bottoms of the pilasters which so far have been merely standing in place unfastened. drive nails through the backing strips (C) into the wall or drill holes for and insert masonry fasteners. The base blocks are then put back with glue. The finished project is shown in Fig. 1-2.

FILL OPEN WALL SPACE WITH A BOOKCASE

Here's an interesting solution to a problem submitted by Beverly Olandt of Rollins, Montana. Olandt has a handsome, ashlar stone planter that divides a living room from a rather dark hallway and

Fig. 1-2. The finished Mantelpiece.

3

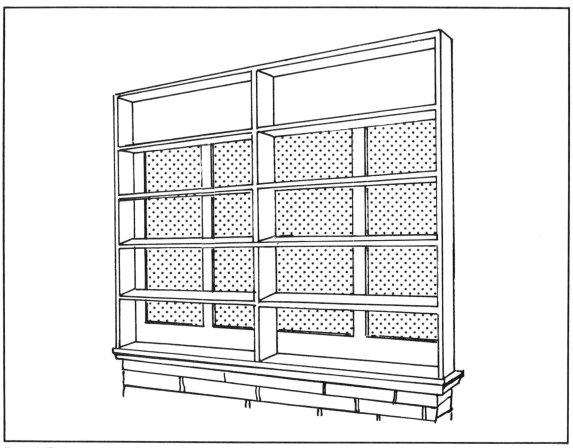

Fig. 1-3. Bookcase as seen from the front.

stairwell (Fig. 1-3). Desiring to fill in the space between the planter and the ceiling, she mounted a bookcase on the planter with a woven cane backing (Fig. 1-4), so that light from the living room could still filter into the dark hallway. She succeeded admirably and here's how she did it.

See Fig. 1-5 and Table 1-2. A single piece of plywood (C) covers the top of the planter. A skirt (D-F) and a rope-shaped half-round molding (J) on the edges of the bottom (C) and all the forward edges of the shelves and verticals (A-H) give the entire project a finished appearance.

The verticals (A) are nailed and glued to the top (B) and bottom (C). They can also be fastened with angle braces that have been countersunk.

The shelves are adjustable and holes are provided in the verticals (A) for the hardware that sup-

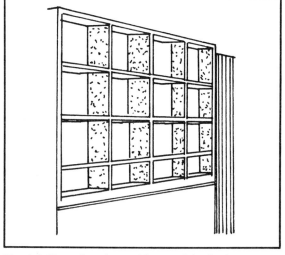

Fig. 1-4. Rear of caning and frame of the Bookcase.

4

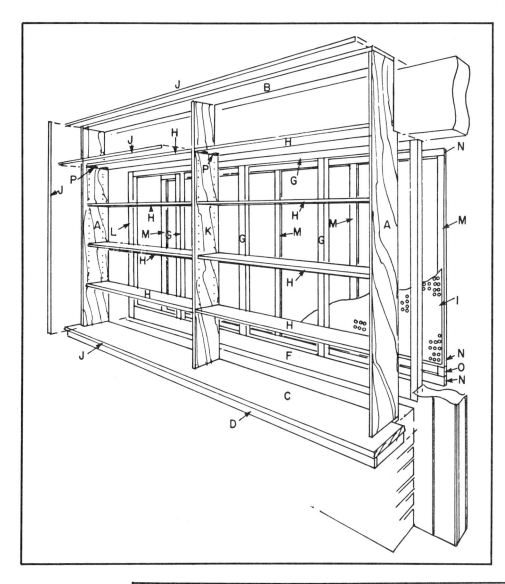

Fig. 1-5. Details of the Bookcase.

Table 1-2. Materials for the Bookcase.

A.	2 pcs, 3/4″ × 9 1/2″ × 69 1/4″	J.	half-round rope turn molding, 67 ft.
B.	1 pc, 3/4″ × 7″ × 93″	K.	1 pc, 3/4″ × 8″ × 69 1/4″
C.	1 pc, 3/4″ × 13 1/2″ × 96″	L.	2 pcs, 1 1/2″ × 1 1/2″ × 53 1/2″
D.	1 pc, 3/4″ × 2″ × 96″	M.	5 pcs, 3/4″ × 1 1/2″ × 46 1/2″
E.	2 pcs, 3/4″ × 2″ × 10″	N.	3 pcs, 3/4″ × 1 1/2″ × 93″
F.	1pc, 1 1/2″ × 5 1/2″ × 90″	O.	5 pcs, 3/4″ × 1 1/2″ × 2 1/2″
G.	3 pcs, 1 1/2″ × 1 1/2″ × 46 1/2″	P.	24 pcs, adjustable shelf supports
H.	8 pcs, 3/4″ × 8″ × 45 3/8″	Q.	1 pc, 1 1/2″ × 1 1/2″ × 90″
I.	4 pcs, 23″ × 96″ caning		

ports them. The top (B) is fastened to the joists overhead with screws that penetrate the plasterboard of the ceiling.

The caning behind the bookcase is supported by a framework of 2 × 2s (G). The four strips of caning are cut slightly larger than the four openings in the framework and stapled along the edges to the back of the frame. A sharp X-acto knife was used to trim ragged edges of caning.

A duplicate frame of 2 × 1s was then fastened with screws and nails to the back of the first frame.

If you are interested in covering a wall opening with framed caning, you do not necessarily need to double the framing as was done here. Wood strips 1/4 inch thick and 1 1/2 inches wide could

be fastened with brads to the back of the frame to hide the staples and cut edges of the caning.

Because the caning tends to stretch in damp weather, it was given two coats of varnish to seal it. Finishing depends on the decor of the room. In this case, the wood was painted with a primer and two coats of enamel. Both coats of enamel were rubbed lightly with steel wool, and the final coat was treated with paste wax.

BUILD A STORAGE COUCH
FOR THE FAMILY ROOM

There are many handsome ways to convert wasted wall/floor space in the family room or den, and this practical storage couch is one of them (Fig. 1-6).

Fig. 1-6. The Storage Couch.

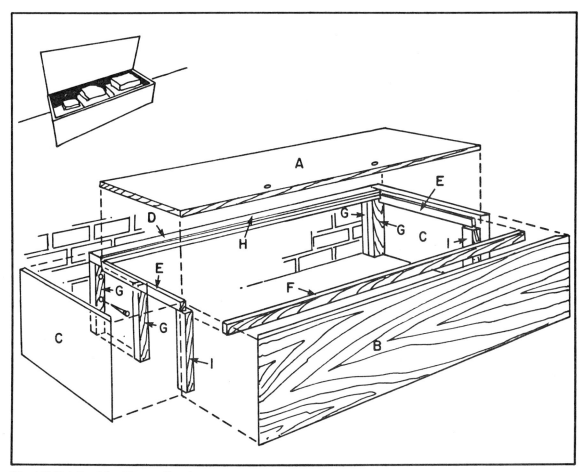

Fig. 1-7. Details of the Storage Couch.

It's a simple piece to make, requiring no more than an afternoon's work. There's ample room in the 3-×-6-foot interior to hold lots of toys, seasonal items, or the family luggage. Papa may find it an ideal spot to recline for his Sunday afternoon snooze.

Refer to Fig. 1-7 and Table 1-3. For structural rigidity, two of the vertical rear supports (G) are firmly anchored to the wall. If the bench is to be built against a brick surface, use lead anchors and lag screws. On wooden-framed walls, fasten one vertical leg to a wall stud using countersunk 3 1/2-inch lag screws and screw the opposite leg to the wallboard with countersunk wallboard anchors.

Next nail the second pair of vertical legs (G) to the already anchored pair and also nail the 2-×-4

rear support (D) in place across the top. Next, mount the seat/lid (A) to the rear support using the long piano hinge. If you cannot find this hinge in

Table 1-3. Materials for the Storage Couch.

A.	1 pc, 3/4″ × 34 5/8″ × 73 1/2″
B.	1 pc, 3/4″ × 16″ × 75″
C.	2 pcs, 3/4″ × 16″ × 39″
D.	1 pc, 1 5/8″ × 3 5/8″ × 73 1/2″
E.	2 pcs, 3/4″ × 1 1/2″ × 33 7/8″
F.	1 pc, 3/4″ × 1 1/2″ × 73 1/2″
G.	4 pcs, 1 5/8″ × 2 5/8″ × 14 3/8″
H.	73 1/2″ piano hinge
I.	2 pcs, 1 5/8″ × 2 5/8″ × 13 3/4″

a 6-foot length, then use two 3-footers. Don't forget the two finger holes for lifting the front of (A). Make them 1 inch in diameter.

The most difficult part is mitering the corners of the side panels (C) and front panel (B) to avoid overlapped joints on the front of the couch. These miters can be accurately cut using a portable jig or circular saw equipped with an angle adjustment. Clamp a straightedge next to the cutting line to guide your saw for a clean, even stroke.

Screw the three support pieces (E) 3/4 inch from the top edges of the side and front panels so that the seat/lid (A) will close flush with these top surfaces. The vertical front supports (I) are screwed to the side panels (C) also from the inside. Finishing nails driven into (I) at both ends hold the front panel (B) in place. These nail heads should be counterset and the holes puttied.

Sand all surfaces and finish the couch using a quality enamel or apply a suitable stain followed by two or more coats of standard or urethane varnish.

The cushion is made of 6-inch foam rubber covered with sail cloth. A zipper in the cushion back permits easy cleaning.

STEP UP TO A BEAUTIFUL BAR

This handsome bar (Fig. 1-8) is an easy do-it-yourself project that results in plenty of counter-top room and drawer and shelf storage space under the counter. The walls of this recreation room were finished in wood-grain paneling colored midnight blue, with matching paneling on the outer end of the bar for a coordinating effect in decoration.

Refer to Fig. 1-9 and Table 1-4. The counter-top (D) was covered with a plastic laminate (A-B-C) which was white with gold speckles.

The basic structure of the bar is a solid piece of plywood backing (BB), recessed base (P, Q), three verticals (U-S-T), and a countertop (D) which overlaps each end vertical (U-T). Therefore, the bar does not necessarily have to be built into the corner of a room but could easily be free-standing in the middle of any free wall you choose. In this case,

Fig. 1-8. The finished Bar.

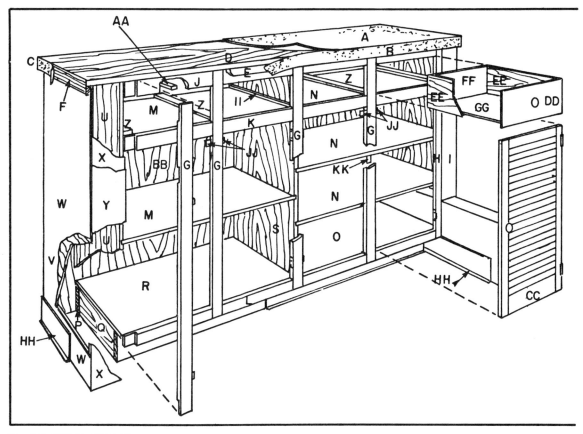

Fig. 1-9. Details of the Bar.

Table 1-4. Materials for the Bar.

A.	1 pc, Formica, 76″ × 21 1/4″	
B.	1 pc, Formica, 76″ × 2″	
C.	1 pc, Formica, 21 1/4″ × 2″	
D.	1 pc, 3/4″ × 76″ × 21 1/4″	
E.	1 pc, 3/4″ × 1 1/4″ × 75 1/4″	
F.	1 pc, 3/4″ × 1 1/4″ × 21 1/4″	
G.	4 pcs, 3/4″ × 2″ × 37 1/4″	
H.	1 pc, 3/4″ × 1 1/4″ × 37 1/4″	
I.	1 pc, 3/4″ × 4″ × 30 1/4″	
J.	1 pc, 3/4″ × 2 1/4″ × 69 1/4″	
K.	1 pc, 3/4″ × 2″ × 69 1/4″	
L.	1 pc, 3/4″ × 1 1/2″ × 65 1/4″	
M.	2 pcs, 1/2″ × 19 1/4″ × 33 3/8″	
N.	3 pcs, 1/2″ × 19 1/4″ × 36 1/4″	
O.	1 pc, 1/2″ × 19 1/4″ × 31 7/8″	
P.	2 pcs, 3/4″ × 5″ × 65 1/4″	
Q.	3 pcs, 3/4″ × 5″ × 14 1/2″	
R.	1 pc, 1/2″ × 19 1/4″ × 33″	
S.	1 pc, 3/4″ × 19 1/4″ × 36 1/4″	
T.	1 pc, 3/4″ × 19 1/4″ × 30 1/4″	
U.	1 pc, 3/4″ × 19 1/4″ × 41 1/4″	
V.	1 pc, 1/2″ × 19 3/4″ × 41 1/4″	
W.	1 pc veneer, 1/4″ × 20 1/2″ × 41 1/4″	
X.	1 pc, 1/2″ × 5 3/4″ × 41 1/4″	
Y.	1 pc, veneer, 1/4″ × 6″ × 41 1/4″	
Z.	4 pcs, 3/4″ × 2″ × 19 1/4″	
AA.	4 pcs, 3/4″ × 1 3/4″ × 19 1/4″	
BB.	1 pc, 1/2″ × 41 1/4″ × 74 1/2″	
CC.	4 pcs, purchased doors, 3/4″ × 14″ × 26″	
DD.	4 pcs, 3/4″ × 5 1/2″ × 14″ 3/4″	
EE.	8 pcs, 1/2″ × 5 1/2″ × 19 3/4″	
FF.	4 pcs, 1/2″ × 5 1/2″ × 13″	
GG.	4 pcs, 3/16″ × 13 1/2″ × 19	
HH.	4″ rubber or vinyl baseboard	
II.	2 pcs, 5/8″ × 3/4″ × 19 1/4″	
JJ.	4 pcs, magnetic catches	
KK.	6 pcs, 1 1/2″ angle braces	

the parts of the bar below the overhang at left and right were concealed with a fill-in piece (I) that sits on the raised step and a front and side piece (X-V) at the other end to make the bar fill the corner completely. Rubber baseboard (HH) is glued around the base of the bar to match wall baseboards which go all around the room.

To begin construction, the bottom frame (P-Q) is nailed and glued to 1/2-inch plywood backing (BB) and covered with the bottom shelf pieces (R-O), allowing a 4-inch toe recess and groove for the middle vertical (S) to be nailed and glued in place. The three main verticals (U-S-T) are secured by nailing through the backing (BB) into the edges of the verticals. The extra vertical (V) is nailed to the backing (BB) in the same manner; the frontal fill-in piece (X) is nailed on; and both pieces (V-X) are covered with 1/4-inch paneling (W-Y) which matches the walls of the room. The 3/4-inch plywood countertop (D) is nailed and glued to the top edges of the verticals (V-U-S-T) and backing (BB), and wood strips (E-F) are added, which— along with the edges of the countertop (D)—provide a 2-inch wide base for the 2-inch wide plastic laminate edging (B,C).

The verticals (U-S-T) are dadoed to receive the edges of three shelves (M-N-N) and two solid pieces of 1/2-inch plywood (M-N) on which the drawers slide. Each of the three shelves (M-N-N) is additionally supported by small right angle braces (KK) on their undersides and attached to the front framing verticals (G-H) and the backing (BB).

The front framing consists of rails (J-K-L) and stiles (G-H) fitted together with *half lap joints*, points at which they are cut to half their thickness and overlap so that they come together flush. Note that the bottom rail (L) provides an overhang so that only the bottom part of the rubber baseboard's full width is visible.

The drawers are kept in place with side guides (Z-II). Strips of wood (AA) attached front and back to the top rail (J) and backing (BB), as well as positioned in the middle of the drawer opening area and flush with the bottom edge of the top rail (J), prevent the drawers from tilting when they are pulled far out. Drawer construction is standard with a 3/4-inch thick front (DD) and 1/2-inch thick sides (EE) and back (FF), all grooved to receive a 3/16-inch thick bottom (GG). Bottom edges of the drawer front, back, and sides should be waxed for easy movement.

Finally, the louver doors (CC), available in building supply stores, are hinged as shown in Fig. 1-9. Note also the magnetic catches (JJ).

BUILD A ROOM DIVIDER

Here's an easy do-it-yourself construction project that will allow you to section off a portion of your living room with an attractive room divider (Fig. 1-10).

Refer to Fig. 1-11 and Table 1-5. The frame (A) of this floor-to-ceiling divider is made of 2 × 4s (1 1/2 × 3 1/2 actual) with mitered ends held together with finishing nails and glue. The round bars (F) are simply 1-inch dowels which fit into holes in the frame and are held there just by glue. Although the frame shown is 8 feet square, these measurements can, of course, be changed to suit any height and length you desire.

Nor, for that matter, do the decorative wooden knobs have to be the same as the ones shown; whatever kind that suit your taste are fine, providing they have 1-inch sections on the bottom which will fit into holes in the frame for the dowels (Detail 2).

The central panel is simply a pair of 2 × 4s (B) covered front and back with 3/8-inch plywood (E). Be sure to center the inside strips (C-D) (Detail 1) so that you allow a 3/8-inch step on each side for the plywood panels to lie flush.

Notice also that strips of wood (G) (lower one, not shown) are used as braces and are toenailed into place. These braces help to stiffen the center area of the plywood when the plywood is nailed to the strips.

Finally, the covering over the plywood panels may be wallpaper, fabric, paint—whatever you wish to harmonize with the decor of the room.

ADD A CORNER BENCH, COFFEE TABLE, AND CABINET

With everything in sight so nicely covered by

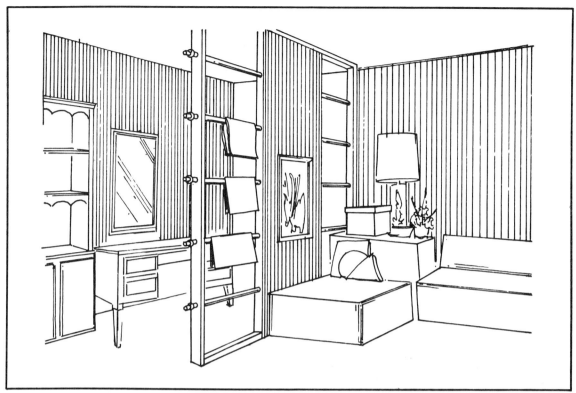

Fig. 1-10. The Room Divider.

Weyerhaeuser's Rusticana Natural Pecan wall paneling, it is hard to believe that there is so much storage space hidden in the scene in Fig. 1-12. Actually, the coffee table, the cabinet at the end of the bench, and the space under the bench provide a great deal of space for storage.

Let's examine the coffee "table," which looks like a set of stacked boxes (Fig. 1-13 and Table 1-6). It is really two large boxes made of 1/2-inch plywood covered with pecan wall paneling, which is fastened to the plywood with panel cement and brads driven through the black scoring. The boxes have mitered corners fastened with glue and reinforced inside with 3-inch right angle braces.

The covers overlap the sides slightly and are edged with thin strips of wood stained to match the pecan paneling on the covers and sides. There are 1 × 1 cleats on the undersides of the covers on all four sides to hold them firmly in place. The covers are not hinged and are simply lifted to open the box.

The cabinet on the left side of the bench is made in the same way as the coffee table. Its top can also be lifted for storage.

The bench has a framework of 2 × 2s put together with nails and glue. The front of the bench is covered with the same kind of paneling seen on the walls and is fastened to the framework with panel cement and colored finishing nails.

The top seat of the bench is made of 3/4-inch plywood and is also covered with paneling. The forward edge of the seat paneling extends beyond the plywood beneath it enough to be flush with the front paneling of the bench. The edge is painted black to match the random scoring of the paneling.

The top, or seat, of the bench is cut into two sections on both sides of the corner. All four seat sections can be lifted to make use of the storage space beneath them. The sections can be hinged at the back, but if you do so, you have to lift them by the 1/4-inch paneling edge in front, which means

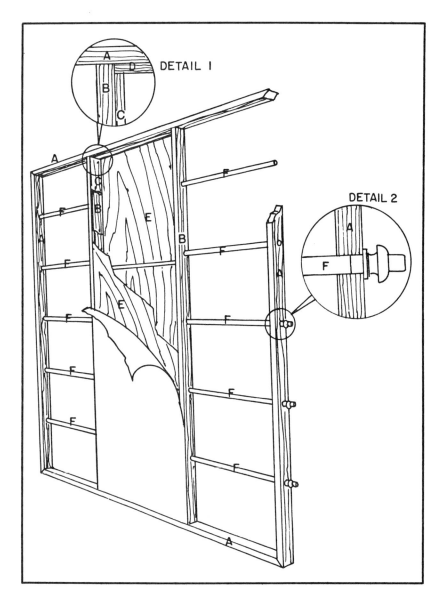

DETAIL I

DETAIL 2

Fig. 1-11. Details of the Room Divider.

Table 1-5. Materials for the Room Divider.

A.	4 pcs, 3 1/2" × 1 1/2" × 8'	
B.	2 pcs, 3 1/2" × 1 1/2" × 7'9"	
C.	2 pcs, 3/4" × 2 3/4" × 77 1/2" (1 pc. not shown)	
D.	2 pcs, 3/4" × 2 3/4" × 3' (1 pc. not shown)	
E.	2 pcs, 3' × 7'9" × 3/8"	
F.	10 pcs, 1" × 2'5 1/4" dowel	
G.	2 pcs, 3/4" × 2 3/4" × 2'9" (1 pc. not shown)	

Fig. 1-12. The Corner Bench, Coffee Table, and Cabinet.

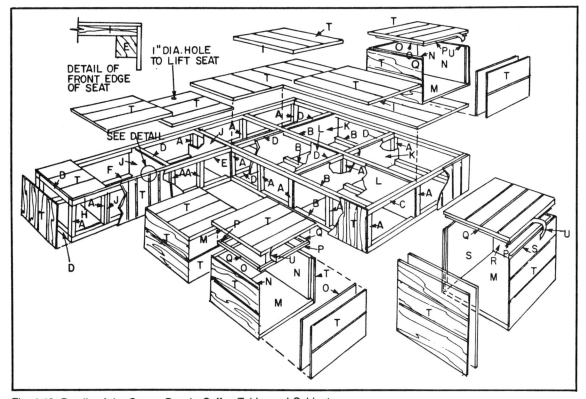

DETAIL OF
FRONT EDGE
OF SEAT

1" DIA. HOLE
TO LIFT SEAT

SEE DETAIL

Fig. 1-13. Details of the Corner Bench, Coffee Table, and Cabinet.

13

A.	22 pcs, 1 1/2″ × 1 1/2″ × 13″
B.	6 pcs, 1 1/2″ × 1 1/2″ × 81″
C.	2 pcs, 1 1/2″ × 1 1/2″ × 48″
D.	14 pcs, 1 1/2″ × 1 1/2″ × 21 3/4″
E.	2 pcs, 1 1/2″ × 1 1/2″ × 74″
F.	2 pcs, 1 1/2″ × 1 1/2″ × 122″
G.	1 pc, 3/4″ × 48″ × 84″
H.	1 pc, 3/4″ × 14″ × 24″
I.	4 pcs, 3/4″ × 24″ × 30″
J.	3 pcs, 3/4″ × 16″ × 24″
K.	2 pcs, 3/4″ × 16″ × 48″
L.	2 pcs, 3/4″ × 16″ × 29 1/4″
M.	8 pcs, 1/2″ × 24″ × 24″
N.	6 pcs, 1/2″ × 16″ × 23″
O.	6 pcs, 1/2″ × 16″ × 24″
P.	8 pcs, 1/2″ × 1/2″ × 23″
Q.	8 pcs, 1/2″ × 1/2″ × 22″
R.	2 pcs, 1/2″ × 23″ × 24″
S.	2 pcs, 1/2″ × 23″ × 23″
T.	wall paneling
U.	edge tape

conspicuous finger marks and possible chipping of the edge.

To avoid this problem, bore two 3/4-inch finger holes in each section at the back, where they will be concealed by the pillows. The finger holes will permit easy lifting of the sections. To prevent any looseness or movement of these sections, nail cleats to their undersides in the spaces between the 2 × 2s that support the seat sections.

MAKE A PROFESSIONAL-LOOKING STORAGE WALL

Here's a very good-looking storage wall with a lot of capacity for almost anything you'd like to put in a living room or basement recreation room (Fig. 1-14). At first glance it looks like a job that could only be done by a professional cabinetmaker. Once you examine it closely, however, you'll discover that it is amazingly simple to assemble.

Basically, it consists of individual cabinet modules, 2 feet wide and 8 feet high, which are fastened to each other to form one storage wall (Fig. 1-15 and table 1-7). The solid cabinet doors (G-H) are made of 3/4-inch plywood with birch veneer on both sides. The verticals (C-B) that make up the cabinet sides are also 3/4-inch plywood, but have birch veneer on only one side. These verticals are held together by the fixed shelves (P-F-E) fastened with glue and nails driven through the sides.

A 3/8-inch plywood back (K) veneered on one side only braces each module and provides rigidity. Each cabinet is attached to its neighbor with 1 1/4-inch flathead screws driven through opposite

Fig. 1-14. The Storage Wall.

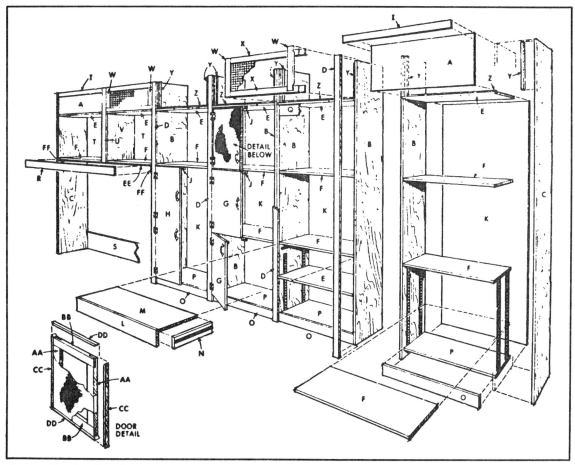

Fig. 1-15 Details of the Storage Wall.

A.	4 pcs, 3/8″ × 13″ × 22 1/2″	Q.	1 pc, 3/8″ × 3″ × 22 1/2″
B.	8 pcs, 3/4″ × 15 1/4″ × 96″	R.	1 pc, 3/8″ × 3″ × 46 1/2″
C.	2 pcs, 3/4″ × 16″ × 96″	S.	1 pc, 3/8″ × 12″ × 48″
D.	4 pcs, 3/4″ × 1 1/2″ × 96″	T.	2 pcs, 3/8″ × 24″ × 24 3/4″
E.	7 pcs, 3/4″ × 16″ × 22 1/2″	U.	1 pc, 3/4″ × 1 1/2″ × 37 3/4″
F.	10 pcs, 3/4″ × 15 1/4″ × 22 1/2″	V.	1 pc, 3/4″ × 15 1/4″ × 37 3/4″
G.	10 pcs, 3/4″ × 11 1/4″ × 28″	W.	4 pcs, 1/2″ × 1 1/2″ × 13″
H.	2 pcs, 3/4″ × 11 1/4″ × 56″	X.	4 pcs, 1/2″ × 1 1/2″ × 22 1/2″
I.	4 pcs, 1/4″ × 1 1/2″ × 22 1/2″	Y.	12 pcs, 3/4″ × 3/4″ × 13″
J.	11 magnetic latches	Z.	6 pcs, 3/4″ × 3/4″ × 21″
K.	4 pcs, 3/8″ × 24″ × 83″	AA.	20 pcs, 3/4″ × 1 1/2″ × 23 1/2″
L.	1 pc, 3/4″ × 3″ × 22 1/2″	BB.	20 pcs, 3/4″ × 1 1/2″ × 10 3/4″
M.	1 pc, 3/4″ × 15 1/4″ × 22 1/2″	CC.	20 pcs, 1/4″ × 3/4″ × 24″
N.	2 pcs, 3/4″ × 2″ × 15 1/4″	DD.	20 pcs, 1/4″ × 3/4″ × 11 1/4″
O.	4 pcs, 3/4″ × 3″ × 22 1/2″	EE.	1 pc, 3/4″ × 3/4″ × 45″
P.	4 pcs, 3/4″ × 14 1/2″ × 22 1/2″	FF.	2 pcs, 3/4″ × 3/4″ × 3″

Table 1-7. Materials for the Storage Wall.

sides (C-B). A long piece of birch-veneered plywood or solid birch (D) is fastened with nails over the joint where the verticals (C) meet. The nails are set and the holes puttied or filled with wax stick.

The smaller doors (B) are covered with burlap stretched over a frame (AA-BB) with halflap joints that are nailed and glued. The burlap is pulled over the frame and stapled in the back. Note the narrow pieces (CC-DD) that cover the edges of these doors and are nailed over the burlap.

There is a series of panels across the top (A) made of 3/8-inch plywood with birch veneer on one side. These are dummy panels covering empty space. The panels are nailed to small cleats (Y-Z) behind them, which, in turn, are nailed to the verticals (C-B) and to the shelf (E) above the burlap-covered doors. The strips at the top (I) are purely decorative and are nailed to the panels before they are installed.

The two grille sections at the top are openings for air conditioning ducts. These openings can be concealed with dummy panels (A) if you have no ducts in that position.

Some of the shelves are adjustable, but this is a matter of your own preference. It is best not to make too many of the shelves adjustable because these members hold the cabinet sides together.

In addition to the cleats on the floor and ceiling which help to anchor the storage wall in place, put some 2-inch flathead screws through the back (K) into the studs behind the plasterboard. Finishing is a matter of taste. Very light birch stain followed by a coat of wax will look fine.

BUILD YOUR OWN TV/HI-FI CONSOLE

Why spend hundreds of dollars for a TV/hi-fi console when you can take the television and hi-fi that you have now and build your own cabinet with separate compartments to house them? Although the console shown in Fig. 1-16 looks as if it were made of fine hardwood, it is actually made from plywood which was painted and then artificially antiqued with an antiquing kit available at many hardware, paint, and department stores.

The construction is very easy because the cabinet is simply an open box structure with divider panels and doors (Fig. 1-17 and Table 1-8). Start by securing cleats (F)—to which the divider panels (B,C) will be attached—to the bottom and top panels (A) with glue and screws. Only one cleat at the top and one at the bottom is needed for each panel.

Five of the six divider panels (B) are glued and screwed into place flush with the rear edge of the bottom panel (A) and 3/4 inch in from the front edge. The sixth partition (C) is also set flush with the rear edge, but is more narrow than the other divider panels (B) to allow room for the front stringers (J).

The two center panels (B,C) are notched so that the top and bottom rear stringers (D) will be flush with the backs of these panels. These stringers (D) are secured with cleats (K) to the bottom (A). The four front stringers (J) are set in 3/4 inch from the front edges of the divider panels (B) to permit the doors (E) to close against them.

At this point, you may wish to modify the basic frame as it is given by adding a back panel to the three main compartments in order to have a fully dustproof construction. Note that the design as shown does already allow for panels (H) at the rear of the two speaker compartments. Only screws are used for the installation of these two rear panels (H) to permit quick and easy accessibility to the speakers.

The four vertical cleats (G) inside each of the speaker compartments are attached 3/4 inch in from the panels' (B) front or back edges with this method, the rear panels (H) and the frames (I) with grille cloth stapled to them fit flush with the edges of the panels (B).

Screen molding, 1/4 × 3/4 inch, (T) is used on the front and side edges of the top and bottom panels (A), as well as on the front edges of the partition panels (B). Glue and brads are used to secure the molding. The trim (T) is mitered at the corners of the top and bottom panels (A).

The base (L,M) is nailed together with butt joints centered on the bottom of the base panel (A), and attached to the base panel with glue and screws through cleats (G). One and a half-inch casters (N) are screwed to the bottom panel inside the base

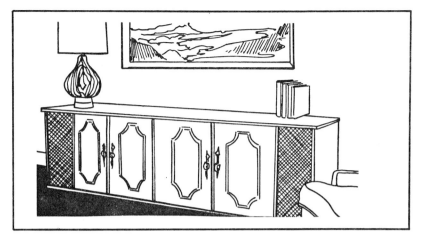

Fig. 1-16. The TV/Hi-Fi Console.

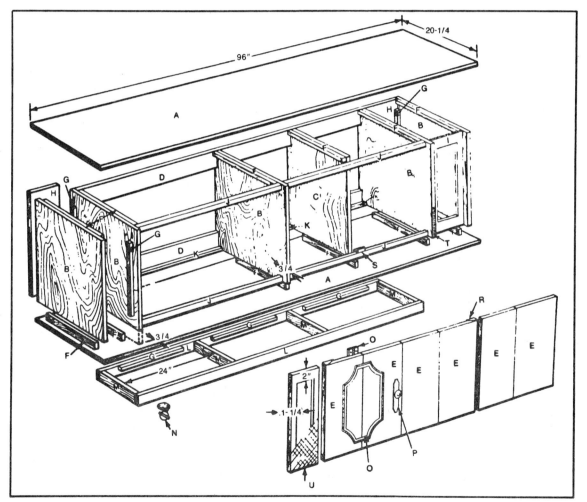

Fig. 1-17. Details of the TV/Hi-Fi Console.

17

A.	2 pcs, 3/4″ × 20 1/4″ × 96″	L.	2 pcs, 3/4″ × 1 3/4″ × 60″
B.	5 pcs, 3/4″ × 19 1/2″ × 23 3/4″	M.	4 pcs, 3/4″ × 1 3/4″ × 13″
		N.	casters
C.	1 pc, 3/4″ × 16″ × 23 3/4″	O.	door panel molding, 2 kits
D.	2 pcs, 3/4″ × 4″ × 74″	P.	4 door pulls
E.	8 pcs, 3/4″ × 9 1/8″ × 23 5/8″	Q.	4 piano hinges
F.	12 pcs, 3/4″ × 1 1/2″ × 15″	R.	8 concealed hinges
G.	14 pcs, 3/4″ × 3/4″ × 18″	S.	2 magnetic catches
H.	2 pcs, 3/4″ × 8 3/4″ × 23 3/4″	T.	screen molding, 1/4″ × 3/4″ × 96″
I.	2 pcs, 1/2″ × 8 5/8″ × 23 5/8″ (centers cut out)	U.	grille cloth
J.	4 pcs, 3/4″ × 1 1/2″ × 36 5/8″		
K.	3 pcs cut to fit from 3/4″ × 3/4″ × 72 1/2″		

Table 1-8. Materials for the TV/Hi-Fi Console.

frame and spread out as much as possible to distribute the weight of the cabinet.

The folding doors (E) are hinged at the outer corners (R) with TV-type invisible hinges and in the center with piano hinges (Q) on each set of doors. Then each pair of doors is hung carefully. Some clearance should be left in fitting the doors to allow for later paint buildup. Use some method of indexing the doors as to their positions on the console (scribing the hinges is one way) so that when you begin painting, you can identify which doors go where. When the doors are satisfactorily hung, molding (O) for the doors is cut to size, positioned, pinned with brads, and glued. Decorative wood or plastic trimming is available in many hardware or building supply stores.

The final step is to very lightly sand all surfaces and apply two coats of semi-gloss enamel. Then the base coat of an antiquing kit should be applied, preferably two coats. Some plywood grain will show through even after the painting, but it enhances the antiquing effect. Then apply the antique glaze and wipe to the grain desired, following the directions on the antiquing kit. The application of two coats of varnish, supplied in most antiquing kits, completes the project.

Chapter 2

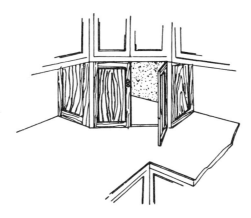

Kitchen/Dining Room Projects

Now that you've improved your living room and/or family room, it's on to the kitchen and dining room! The projects in this chapter are sure to win your heart as they help you to conserve space, add beauty, and increase the usefulness of your kitchen and dining room.

MAKE YOUR OWN PASS-THROUGH

Cutting through a partition wall to make an opening, which for want of a better term you can call a *pass-through*, is really quite easy. Such an opening is often more desirable for serving drinks or food to guests than a doorway or archway through which you or your wife can be seen working in the kitchen, especially when you can close the opening with attractive wooden shutters as shown in Fig. 2-1.

Refer to Fig. 2-2 and Table 2-1. The first thing you should do is to make certain whether or not the wall through which you are going to cut is load-bearing. If it is, put up temporary bracing from ceiling to floor in the from of a 2 × 4 on both sides

of the wall. If you are not certain, do it anyway to be safe.

Measure the width and height of shutters carefully. Allow for a 3/4-inch facing (C-E-D) on both sides and top of the opening.

Cut through the plasterboard and studs with an electric saber saw or a fine-toothed handsaw. You will have to cut away more plasterboard on the reverse side of the wall, as shown in Fig. 2-2, to give yourself room to install the double (F) 2 × 4s at the top of the opening and the single one at the bottom (F). They should be toenailed at the ends to the existing studs at the sides and nailed straight to the center, or cut, stud. Check with a carpenter's level to be certain that the new horizontals are square.

New strips of plasterboard should be nailed in place to replace those removed from the reverse or kitchen, side of the opening to cover the new horizontals. The cracks should be plastered and sanded. Repainting of the entire reverse wall will probably be necessary.

The sill (D) must be notched at each end. It is

Fig. 2-1. The Pass-Through.

dropped into place before the moldings (A-B-A) and the facings (C-E-C) are installed. Both the moldings and facings should be fastened with finishing nails that are counterset. The nail holes should be filled with wood putty.

With the opening finished, primed and painted, chisel out shallow recesses in the facings to allow the shutter hinges to lie flush when fastened with screws.

REPLACE KITCHEN COUNTERS YOURSELF

Installing a new counter is an inexpensive way to add new pizzazz to a kitchen. Here's how you can do it yourself in 10 easy steps.

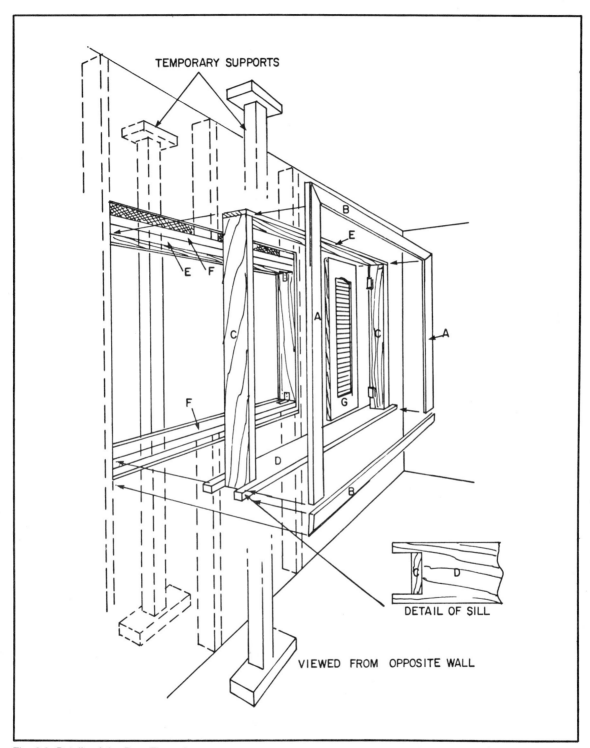

TEMPORARY SUPPORTS

DETAIL OF SILL

VIEWED FROM OPPOSITE WALL

Fig. 2-2. Details of the Pass-Through.

21

Table 2-1. Materials for the Pass-Through.

A.	4 pcs, 3/4″ × 2″ × 22 1/4″
B.	4 pcs, 3/4″ × 2″ × 32 1/2″
C.	2 pcs, 1 1/4″ × 4 1/2″ × 21″
D.	1 pc, 1″ × 6 1/2″ × 34 1/4″
E.	1 pc, 3/4″ × 4 1/2″ × 30 1/2″
F.	3 pcs, 1 1/2″ × 3 1/2″ × 30 1/2″
G.	4 doors, 3/4″ × 7″ × 20″

If you've been thinking that installing a new counter in your kitchen is beyond the modestly equipped do-it-yourselfer, there is good news for you. With a few supplies and a bit of carpentry, you can complete the job in a weekend at a fraction of remodeling costs.

New replacement countertops available are prefabricated and offer durable laminated plastic surfaces. Brand name countertops come in a wide range of colors and patterns. You can find them at building supply firms.

Measure First

Before you buy a new countertop, first make a layout of the one you plan to replace. Some tips: Measure accurately along the wall at the cabinet top level to get the exact length of counter top sections required. When measuring, keep in mind that for end overhang on an exposed counter end, 3/4 inch is normally added.

You'll need End Cap kits to cover ends that will be exposed (or where appliances will not cover the end completely). Likewise you'll need End Splash kits to use where countertops butt a wall. When using End Splash kits, deduct 3/4 inch from the overall top dimensions.

What to Buy

After measuring, you're ready to head to your building supply dealer. First find the counter top in the color and style that suits you. If you need either L- or U-shaped countertops, it's best to have

Fig. 2-3. The original kitchen, with the old kitchen counter in place.

the miter cuts done professionally. If you need miter cuts, don't forget to buy connector kits to hold the sections of counter together.

Make sure you get End Cap and/or End Splash installation kits to match. Other materials to get, if you don't have them, include tub caulking compound, wood screws, masking tape, nails, and glue. You'll also want to buy or rent tools you don't have: claw hammer, fine-toothed saw, file, level, keyhole or saber saw, drill, straight edge, tape measure, screwdriver, saw horses, open-end wrench for connector kits, and protective eyewear. Note: For End Cap kit installation, you'll also need a clothes iron.

Replacing the Counter

With tools and materials on hand, you are ready to begin. But before starting the installation, make absolutely sure that electric power and water sources are cut off completely. Remove the sink and/or range if they are located on the cabinet surface to be replaced. Then follow these steps, in order.

• Regardless of the material it is made of (steel, tile, laminated plastic, etc.), your old countertop has been secured to the cabinet with screws, glue, or nails (Fig. 2-3). This old countertop must be removed. First check inside the cabinet for screws or nails that may be attached to the old top and remove them. Then, as gently as possible, pry the countertop away from the cabinet with a lifting action. Try first to simply lift the countertop off the cabinet. You many need to use a wedge and a hammer for better leverage. Be certain that you do not splinter or damage the cabinet base when removing the old countertop.

• Once the old countertop has been removed, check the cabinet to ensure that it is level. If any section needs to be raised, use a small wooden wedge or shim between the floor and the base of the cabinet to make it level.

• Cut the countertop length first (Fig. 2-4). Place the counter top, with the surface side up, on the saw horses. Put a piece of masking tape on the area to be cut and, using a straightedge, mark the line with a pencil on the tape to help prevent surface chipping and give a smooth, finished end. Use

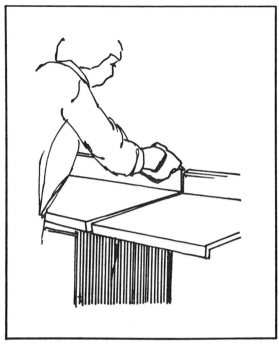

Fig. 2-4. Cut the new counter-top length with a fine-toothed saw.

a fine-toothed saw (10 or 12 pts.) and cut into the surface through the tape.

• To determine the exact placement for the sink or range—if required—remeasure that section first from one end to the center of the sink and from the opposite end to the center of the sink. These measurements should be along the wall behind the counter. They will give you the left to right center of the sink cutout. The cutout area from back to front should be centered or exactly the same as the dimensions of your old countertop and should be measured very accurately.

Now, place the countertop on the saw horses, back side up. Mark the sink or range cutouts by laying the sink rim or range top rim on the back side of your new countertop in the proper position. Mark completely around the outside edge of the rim. Now measure 1/4 inch on all four sides and, using a straightedge, make a complete new perimeter 1/4 inch inside the original sink rim mark. Cut the sink or range cutout using the inside perimeter. If you are installing a self-rimmed stainless steel sink, mark around the outer edge of the sink and make the cutting perimeter 1/4 inch smaller, as just described.

After marking, measure again to make certain that the area cutout is small enough so the sink or range top rim fits on the countertop and the entire unit does not fall through the cutout.

After the lines have been marked and checked again for the sink or range cutout, drill through the countertop in one corner area where the cutout is to be made. Drill a hole from the back side but an inch or two inside the cutout area so that if the drilling scars the finished surface, it will be in the cutout area and will not mar the surface that will be exposed. (The only purpose for this hole is to have a starting place for the saw blade.) Now use a saber saw or keyhole saw and cut along the lines you have marked (Fig. 2-5). For sink and range cutouts, cut from the back side of the countertop where marked. Cutting may produce a slightly rough edge on the counter surface, but the sink or range rim will cover it when installed.

• Now finish the ends of your countertop, using either an End Cap kit (for exposed countertop ends) (Fig. 2-6) or an End Splash kit for counter ends that butt against a wall. Complete instructions are provided with each kit.

End Cap kits have preadhesive backing, and with the use of a household iron this cap adheres readily to finish the exposed end (Fig. 2-7) To prevent blistering or damage, put masking tape over the end cap surface before ironing. Afterwards, remove masking tape.

Included with End Cap kits are buildup strips. Nail these strips to the under side of countertop and back side of the back splash. They provide additional support for the end cap. End Splash finishing is done with screws, and instructions included with the kit should be followed (Fig. 2-8).

• If the new countertop is to be L- or U-shaped, precut miters should be joined now. These miters should be cut by the dealer where you bought the countertop. You should also get a connector kit for each miter joint (Fig. 2-9). Complete instructions for joining the miters are included in the connector kit. Using these instructions, assemble the miter sections at this time.

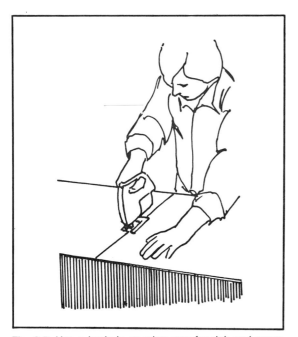

Fig. 2-5. Use a keyhole or saber saw for sink and range cutouts.

Fig. 2-6. Build-up strips add support to End Caps for the exposed end.

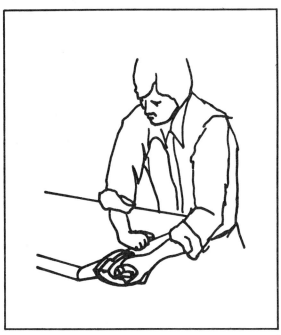

Fig. 2-7. End Caps are ironed on, using tape to prevent blistering.

• Now place your new countertop section in position on the cabinet top and check to make sure the top cabinet drawers and under counter appliances have sufficient clearance for opening. If the new countertop overhang restricts the movement of these drawers or appliances, it will be necessary to build up the countertop. To do so, use 3/4- × -2- × -2-inch wooden support pads (or blocks) and glue or nail these blocks to the front and back of the countertop about every 2 feet (Fig. 2-10).

• Now place the new countertop on the cabinet against the back walls so that the back splash is flush against the wall. If this back wall is not straight, there will be gaps, which will need to be corrected. To do so, place a sharp pencil flat against the wall and vertically, with the pencil point on top of the back splash of the countertop. Scribe a line directly on this back splash. If the pencil line is irregular, you'll need to sand or file the back side of the back splash—toward the marked line—where necessary to ensure a flush wall fit.

• Now the countertop is ready for attachment

Fig. 2-8. End Splash kits, for ends that butt walls, attach with screws.

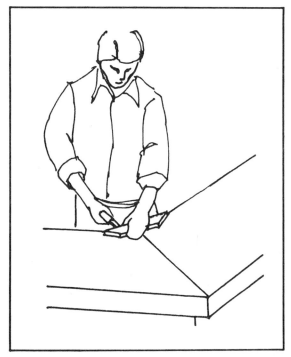

Fig. 2-9. Precut miters for L- or U-shaped tops are joined with a miter Connector Kit.

Fig. 2-10. Support pads are used on the underside if build-up is needed for drawer or door clearance.

to the cabinet. First, run a ribbon of glue down the length of the cabinet top front and back. Position the top carefully on the glued area and set down. To ensure stabilization, you may wish to use wood screws from the inside of the cabinet up into the countertop. Be sure to check the length of these screws to make sure they won't protrude through the countertop surface. (Screws can best be used in corner areas, particularly if triangular blocks are used in the cabinet corners.)

To waterproof the crevice between the wall and the edge of the countertop, use a ribbon of rubber caulking compound.

• A clamp-type sink rim is normally used to install your sink. Complete instructions should come with your sink rim. To waterproof, use a good, thick ribbon of rubber caulking compound or plumber's putty on the areas where the sink rim fits on the countertop. (Be sure to use caulking or putty heavily to seal. The excess can be wiped away.)

If your old sink does not have a sink-mounted faucet, it is better to replace the sink rather than cut out individual faucet holes in your new countertop. The range top (if it has been removed) should be replaced in the same way as the sink, in its same position and reconnected as before. Your new countertop should now be in position and sink and range should be in place (Fig. 2-11). Remove any excess glue and caulking compound from all areas.

Although your new laminated plastic counter-top is unaffected by boiling water, alcohol, fruit acids, and most normal household chemicals, you should avoid using strong bleaches and very abrasive cleaners. You should also avoid placing hot cooking utensils taken directly from the stove on the counter top. Lighted cigarettes can also blister or scorch it.

USE SPACE WISELY
WITH THIS BREAKFAST BAR

Careful use of openings between adjoining rooms in your house can vastly increase the space you have. This space can be multiplied even more with the addition of a sliding table, such as this pass-through breakfast bar features (Fig. 2-12).

The sliding table feature can be used as a handy work surface to prepare breakfast and then be instantly converted into a convenient breakfast nook area. The convenience doesn't end there—the cabinets are designed to give you access to them from either side. You can increase the efficiency of this arrangement even more by arranging whatever you store in these cabinets on single-layered lazy Susan hardware. They can be bought for very little money and give quick and total access to these items from either side of the pass-through. Inclusion of a multilayered lazy Susan in the left-hand side of Fig. 2-13, is there simply to indicate one of the many possible design changes which will help you increase the usefulness of this pass-through breakfast bar. No dimensions are given for this item in Table 2-2, however, because they may vary widely among manufacturers.

Soft indirect lighting of both the kitchen and breakfast nook areas is provided by fluorescent lamps (AB) installed on top of the cabinet. If you

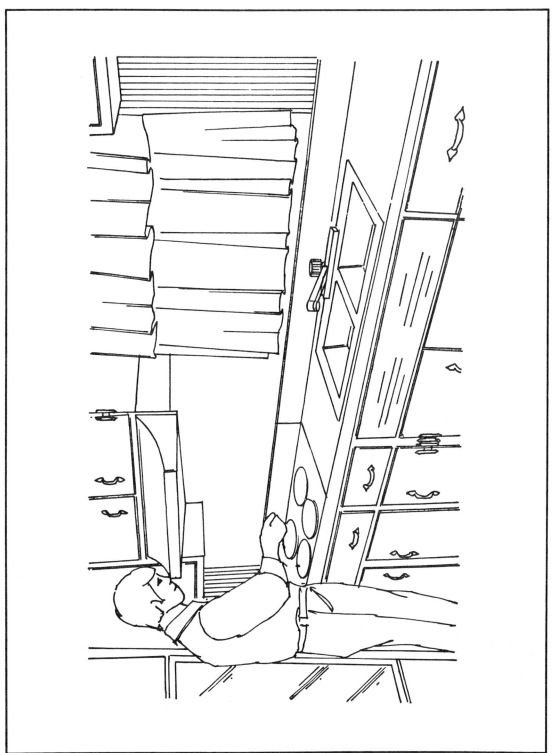

Fig. 2-11. The new counter top, after sink and range surface units are replaced. Excess glue and caulking compound is removed from all areas.

Fig. 2-12. The Breakfast Bar.

use Plexiglas or some other translucent material in place of the solid stock called for (AC) at the top of the cabinet, you can have additional lighting for the cabinets.

Plywood, some with hardwood veneer on one side, is widely used in building this project, although the basic frame of both the upper and lower cabinets are of 1-×-2 stock. Hardboard (I,J,P,S) is also used, as a 4 × 4s for legs of the sliding table. The major uprights are generally held in place by small angle-iron brackets (EE).

Birch veneer tape (AG, AH), used to cover the edge grain of the plywood, should be sanded or shaved down for a perfect fit. Future maintenance of the counters and table is cut down by the use of plastic laminate. The laminated plastic sheet covering the rabbeted corners of the table legs should be mitered to hide the joint, as shown in Fig. 2-13.

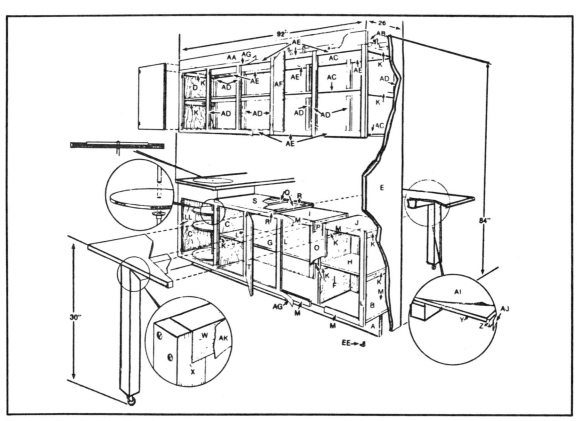

Fig. 2-13. Details of the Breakfast Bar.

Table 2-2. Materials for the Breakfast Bar.

A.	1 base, 90 1/2" × 4" × 1"		W.	1 pc, 64" × 4" × 4"
B.	1 pc, 90 1/2" × 22" × 3/4"		X.	2 pcs, each: 26" × 4" × 4"
C.	2 pcs, each: 30" × 22" × 3/4"		Y.	1 pc, 66" × 33 1/4" × 1"
D.	1 pc, 30" × 22" × 3/4"		Z.	2 pcs, each: 66" × 2" × 1" (1 not shown)
E.	1 pc, 80" × 24" × 3/4"		AA.	2 pcs, each: 91 1/4" × 5" × 1" (1 not shown)
F.	1 pc, 23" × 22" × 3/4"			
G.	1 pc, 46 7/8" × 22" × 3/4"		AB.	1 fluorescent lamp fixture, 72"
H.	1 pc, 22" × 15 1/2" × 3/4"		AC.	3 pcs, each: 90 1/2" × 24" × 3/4"
I.	1 pc, 46" × 22" × 1/4"			
J.	1 pc, 22" × 14 1/4" × 1/4"		AD.	12 pcs, each: 25" × 2" × 1" (1 not shown)
K.	18 pcs, each: 18" × 2" × 1" (8 not shown)			
			AE.	20 pcs, each: 16" × 2" × 1" (9 not shown)
L.	6 pcs, each: 25" × 2" × 1" (2 not shown)			
			AF.	10 doors, each: 21 1/2" × 16 1/4" × 3/4" (9 not shown)
M.	8 pcs, each: 12" × 2" × 1" (3 not shown)			
			AG.	plywood veneer tape, 1200" × 2 1/2"
N.	8 pcs, each: 14" × 2" × 1" (not shown)			
			AH.	plywood veneer tape, 90" × 26"
O.	2 pcs, each: 25" × 6" × 1"			
P.	3 pcs, each: 24" × 4" × 1/4" (1 not shown)		AI.	plastic laminate, 66" × 33 1/4" × 1/16"
			AJ.	plastic laminate, 135" × 2" × 1/16"
Q.	3 pcs, each: 24" × 2" × 1" (1 not shown)			
			AK.	plastic laminate, 400" × 4" × 1/16"
R.	2 pcs, each: 32" × 2" × 1"			
S.	1 pc, 32" × 26" × 1/4"		EE.	angle irons (number and size variable)
T.	4 doors, each: 23 3/4" × 14 1/4" × 3/4" (3 not shown)			
			LL.	4 pcs, each: 30" × 2" × 1" (2 not shown)
U.	4 doors, each: 23 3/4" × 12 1/4" × 3/4" (not shown)			
V.	1 door, 24 1/4" × 23 3/4" × 3/4" (not shown)			

CONSTRUCT A COFFEE MILL

Grind your own fresh coffee every morning! Whole coffee beans are easily obtained by the pound, and in a variety of blends. The only other item you need is a coffee mill which you can make for yourself (Fig. 2-14).

Why bother to grind your own coffee? Ready ground coffee loses part of its flavor every time it is exposed to air when the can is opened. Stored whole bean coffee loses much less flavor on exposure to air because each bean acts as a separate little container. When you grind it just before using it, you get the most possible delicious flavor.

Construction is simple. Two pieces of 1/2-inch walnut 7 1/2 × 12 inches provide all parts for the box and base. One pieces of 1/4-inch basswood or hardboard 6 × 12 inches is enough for all interior parts of the drawer. Layout the walnut pieces as

Fig. 2-14. The Coffee Mill.

Fig. 2-15. The Coffee Mill is ready for assembly after you cut walnut parts for the box and bass or hardboard parts for the drawer. The drawer front is walnut.

shown in Fig. 2-15, with grain running as indicated. There are no fancy joints to cut. All parts are butt-joined. Cut parts to the sizes given in Table 2-3 with a fine-toothed saw and assemble them with glue (Figs. 2-16 through 2-19).

Drill a center hole in the drawer front to receive the bolt for the drawer pull. In this model a ceramic knob with an eagle design was used.

To install the mill mechanism, put it in place temporarily while you use an awl to mark the locations of screw holes in the sides for fastening the mill (Fig. 2-20). Remove the mill so that you can enlarge the holes by wiggling your awl back and forth.

Before reinstalling the mill, apply clear finish to all surfaces, except the interior of the drawer which should have no finish. It catches the ground coffee from the mill. You may prefer to stain the exterior walnut surfaces with a walnut stain. If you do, allow the wood to dry overnight before applying the clear finish, which can be lacquer, varnish, urethane, or a penetrating type. Again do not stain or finish the interior of the drawer. Paint or gild the grinder knob.

BUILD A TRASH COMPRESSOR

Do your trash cans threaten to explode with overflowing household trash? A lot more could be put into the cans if the trash took up less space;

Table 2-3. Materials for the Coffee Mill.

Cut following parts from 2 pcs of 1/2″ × 7 1/2″ × 12″. Last dimension indicates grain direction:
Front, 2 1/4″ × 5 1/4″
Side, 4 1/2″ × 4 3/4″, 2 pcs
Back, 4 1/2″ × 4 1/4″
Drawer front, 2 1/4″ × 5 1/4″
Base, 5 5/8″ × 5 5/8″

Cut following from 1/4″ × 6″ × 12 1/4″ plywood or hardboard:
Drawer sides, 2 1/4″ × 4 3/16″, 2 pcs
Drawer back, 2 1/4″ × 3/4″
Drawer bottom, 3 3/4″ × 3 15/16″

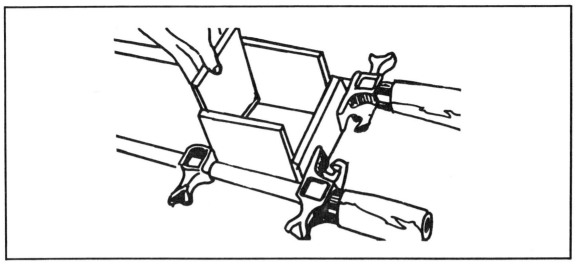

Fig. 2-16. Two bar clamps, with basswood scraps to protect work, are used for the assembly of the front and back to the sides.

eliminate the air pockets in trash bags by compressing each bag. Since most hydraulic presses are so expensive and difficult to operate, however, why not build your own (Fig. 2-21)? One nice feature about this one is that it's tailor-made to contain trash bags which are actually nothing more than

Fig. 2-17. The assembled case serves as a form to hold the butt-joined drawer part square during glue-up. This illustration shows the front part of the drawer being glued.

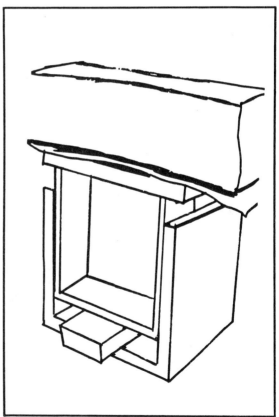

Fig. 2-18. A brick provides pressure on the drawer front while the drawer is held in a square position while the glue hardens.

31

Fig. 2-19. The case with the drawer in place is laid on the base so the gluing guideline can be accurately located. The drawer is removed, and the case is glued to the base.

large grocery bags. The pressure to operate the press is supplied by an automobile bumper-jack (H) mounted as shown in Detail 1 of Fig. 2-22. The jack can apply enough pressure to break bottles, flatten cans, and compress the average bag of trash to as little as 1/4 its original volume.

Exterior plywood 3/4 inch thick is used for all of the wooden parts of the compressor (Table 2-4). The sides (D) are cut considerably wider than the size of the bag. Reinforcing strips (J) are glued to the back edges of the sides to hold the back (I) of

the press.

Detail 2 of Fig. 2-22 shows the pattern used to cut the sides. The top edges of the sides are slotted to receive a wooden bar (K) that holds the front (I) of the compression chamber in place.

Piece C, the bottom of the press, is actually two pieces of wood. The center piece is formed when the slots are cut as shown in Detail 3 of Fig. 2-22 to receive the side pieces and prevent their bulging out when pressure is applied.

Replace the 3/8-inch rivet that holds the

Fig. 2-20. The mill mechanism is dropped into the case, where two screws driven into the top edge of the sides will hold it in place.

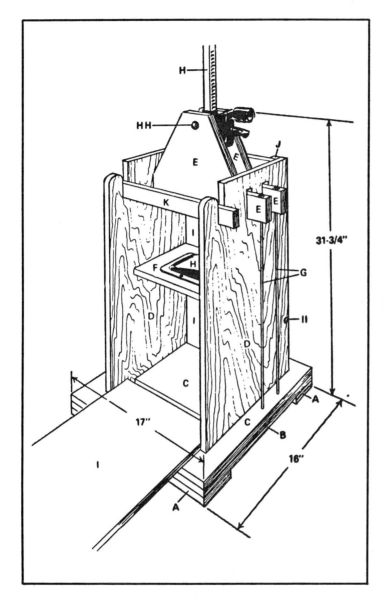

Fig. 2-21. Details of the Trash Compressor.

bumper hook to the jack (H) with a 3/8-inch bolt (HH) that passes through two triangular-shaped pieces (E) on either side of the jack. The rivet can be removed by simply drilling out the end opposite to the head. A sharp 1/4-inch twist bit in your drill will do the job nicely. The triangular pieces extend through the sides (D) and are notched to hold the sides securely in place.

Four threaded 1/4-inch rods (G) plus nuts and washers, connect the triangular pieces with the bot-tom of the press (B,C) to take the strain of com-pression. Piece F, which is almost the same size as the compression chamber, is attached to the foot of the jack with screws.

To operate the compressor, the front (I) is removed by lifting the wooden bar (K) and raising the foot of the jack to its highest position. The bag of trash is inserted; the front is closed and barred; and the jack is operated to move the foot downward to compress the bag. When pressure is released by

33

Table 2-4. Materials for the Trash Compressor.

A.	2 pcs, each: 17″ × 2 1/2″ × 3/4″		8 nuts and washers
B.	1 pc, 17″ × 16″ × 3/4″	H.	1 automobile bumper-jack
C.	1 pc, 17″ × 16″ × 3/4″	I.	2 pcs, each: 24″ × 11″ × 3/4″
D.	2 pcs, each: 24″ × 12″ × 3/4″	J.	2 pcs, each: 24″ × 3/4″ × 3/4″
E.	2 pcs, each: 17″ × 11″ × 3/4″	K.	1 pc, 17″ × 2″ × 3/4″
F.	1 pc, 10 15/16″ × 6 15/16″ × 3/4″	HH.	1 bolt, 4″ × 3/8″ (diameter)
G.	4 threaded rods, each: 24″ × 1/4″,	II.	1 threaded bolt, 13″ × 3/8″ (diameter)

Fig. 2-22. Grids for the parts of the Trash Compressor.

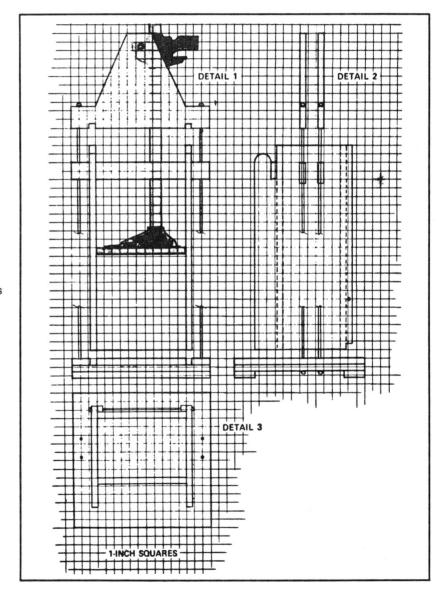

DETAIL 1   DETAIL 2

DETAIL 3

1-INCH SQUARES

34

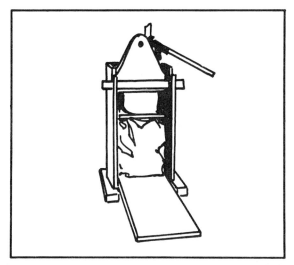

Fig. 2-23. The front view of the opened compressor. A bag of garbage has been inserted between the foot of the jack and the floor of the chamber.

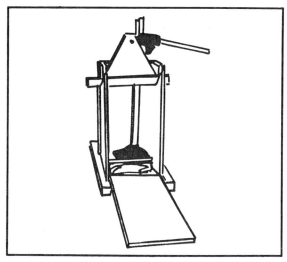

Fig. 2-25. The trash compressor has been reopened, and the volume of garbage has been reduced to one-fourth its original size.

raising the foot, the front is removed again, and the compressed trash is removed. See Figs. 2-23 through 2-27.

Trash cans that can normally hold only three bags of uncompressed trash in each will easily hold six bags of compressed trash. An occasional washing down is about the only maintenance required. You can paint your compressor with a good grade of enamel.

USE THESE CLEVER
STORAGE IDEAS IN YOUR KITCHEN

Any existing kitchen can be made more convenient for the housewife by using some of the following ideas. Very few homeowners have enough storage space in their kitchens, so some of the sketches suggest ways in which you can get more items into the cabinet space you now have.

Other sketches deal with the problem of ac-

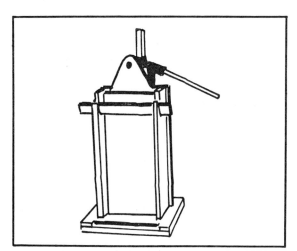

Fig. 2-24. The front of the compression chamber is closed and secured with a wooden bar. The top edges of the sides are slotted to receive the bar.

Fig. 2-26. The rear view of the compressor. Observe the horizontal rod across the back edges. Its purpose is to take the strain of the compression.

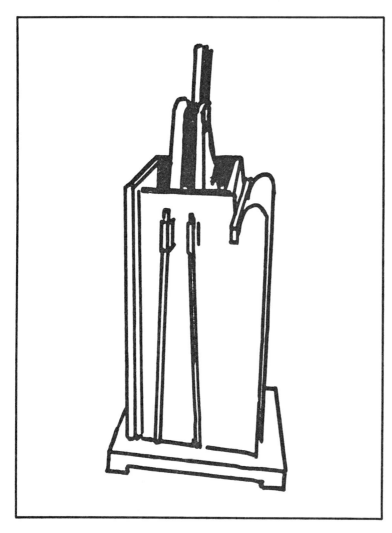

Fig. 2-27. The side view shows two vertical rods which help to relieve pressure. Although not pictured so, they should be straight. A bolt holds the jack to two plywood triangles.

cessibility and convenience. You can always pack a shelf with cans from front to back, but how do you get at the cans in the back without taking out most of the cans in front? There is a particularly difficult problem with items stored in base cabinets. To get at such items, you usually have to get down on your hands and knees and reach all the way into the back. Some simple and ingenious ideas have been suggested to solve this and similar problems.

Sometimes convenient accessibility is well worth the loss of a little storage place, and some of the sketches are based on this idea. Since we are dealing with ideas here, no measurements or lists of materials are given.

Paper Plate and Cup Storage

Many housewives escape the tyranny of washing dishes by making use of paper plates and cups for children's lunches and afternoon snacks with visiting friends. Figure 2-28 shows a very easy project for storing paper plates and cups. The three cup dispensers (E) on each shelf are made of 1/2-inch material. A round section of solid wood glued to E goes up into the bottom cup of each stack of cups, and a single continuous hinge permits all three stacks to tip forward. The box frame (C,B) of each storage unit is made of 5/8-inch plywood, and the partitions (D) are made of 1/2-inch material, while the cup partition is 1/4-inch hardboard. The facing

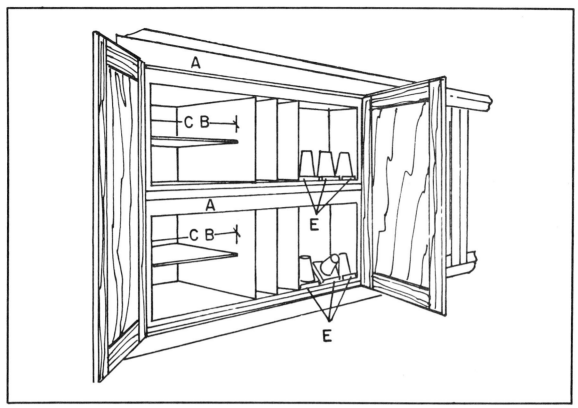

Fig. 2-28. Paper plate and cup storage.

strip (A) is 1/2-inch material.

Spice Rack

You can store more boxes or cans of spices on this rack than by almost any other method, and it swings out very conveniently (Fig. 2-29). The two sides (A) are made of 3/4-inch material, 8 inches wide. The shelves are 1/4-inch plywood about 4 inches wide on both sides of the middle partition (B) and fit into grooves in the sides and partition. The whole rack swings on a continuous hinge the length of A.

Disappearing Chopping Board

The chopping board in Fig. 2-30A is made of glued maple sections 1 1/2 × 2 inches reinforced with two 1/2-inch dowels (D). The front support (B) is 3/4-inch maple 3 inches high. The sliding runners are maple 3/4 × 3 inches (see detail). You can also

use strong, steel extension rollers of the type used in steel filing cabinets. The chopping board slides back and is concealed by a hinged drawer front (E).

Removable Plastic Drawers

As every housewife knows, there is a wealth of plastic drawers or deep (4 inches) trays that can be used to store vegetables and fruits (Fig. 2-31). You can transform an empty base cabinet into a storage center for this purpose by screwing 1/2- × -1/2-inch cleats against the sides of the cabinet. Place the cleats just far enough apart for the lips of the plastic drawers.

Storage for Trays

Everybody has trays that always seem to be too large for easy storage. Then there are also those large serving dishes you only use for big dinners

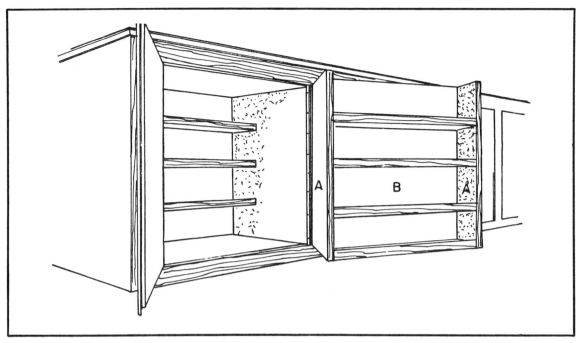

Fig. 2-29. Spice Rack.

which never fit in the china closet. Store them by standing them on end in a base cabinet unit with a grooved 3/4-inch top and bottom (A) with partitions (B) made of 1/8-inch hardboard that slide easily in the grooves (Fig. 2-32).

Storage for Bottles
Storing large beverage bottles is always a problem in the average kitchen but a pull-out shelf like the one shown in Fig. 2-33 makes access to bottles easy. The front (A), sides (B), and back (E) are all

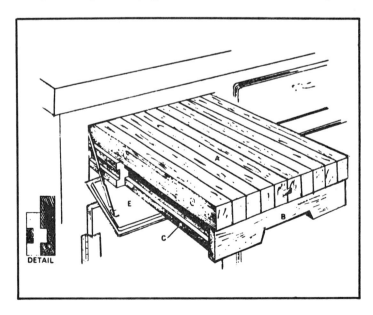

Fig. 2-30. A disappearing chopping board.

Fig. 2-31. Removable plastic drawers.

3/4-inch thick and 3 inches high. The bottom (D) is made of 1/2-inch plywood, as is the top (C), which has the holes for bottles. The whole unit rides on steel extension drawer rollers.

Sliding Shelves

To get at anything stored in most under-the-counter cabinets requires deep bending, squatting, or getting down on hands and knees. Solve this problem by mounting the shelves on extension drawer rollers (Fig. 2-34D). When you pull out the shelf, you have complete access to its contents without reaching. In the drawing, the shelf (B) is 3/4 inch thick, and the sides (A) and back (C) are strips 3/4 × 3 inches high.

Handy Cabinet For Small Items

Every kitchen needs a minicabinet for small items, such as pencils, writing paper, telephone lists, flashlights, etc. that just don't fit elsewhere. You can make it out of plywood with a birch or other veneer to match your kitchen cabinets and screw it to the underside of a wall cabinet, perhaps above the counter where you have a phone (Fig. 2-35). Use plastic tracks for sliding hardboard or plastic doors.

Sliding Baskets For Vegetables

All sorts of wire baskets can be found at many home furnishings stores. Pick a type that has a protruding lip along the sides that can slide in grooved movable runners (Fig.2-36A) 1 inch thick and 1 3/4 inches wide. The runner can be made of three pieces and should have a tongue in front and back to fit into notched verticals (B). The basket can be used for vegetables and is easily removed and replaced.

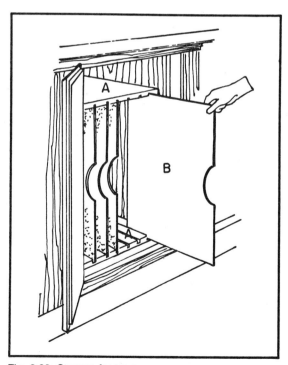

Fig. 2-32. Storage for trays.

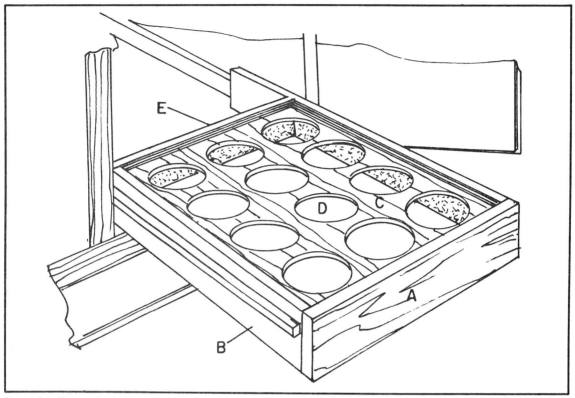

Fig. 2-33. Storage for bottles.

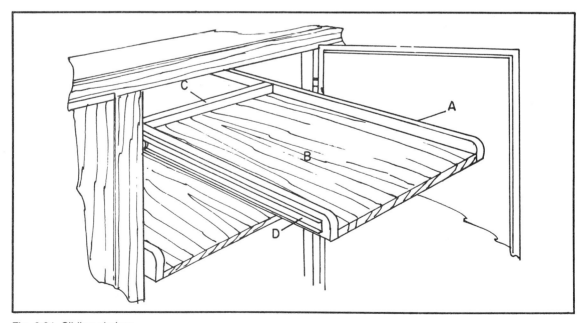

Fig. 2-34. Sliding shelves.

40

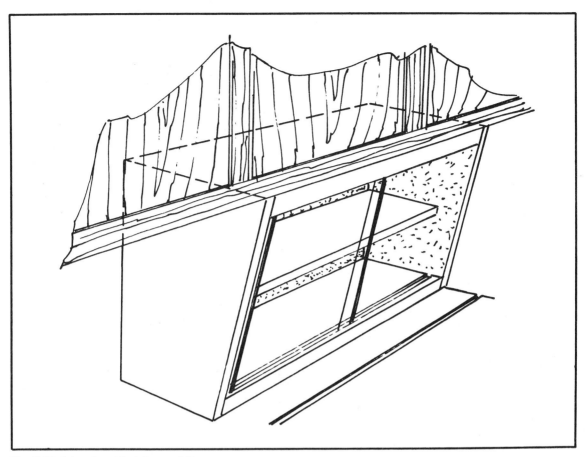

Fig. 2-35. A handy cabinet for small items.

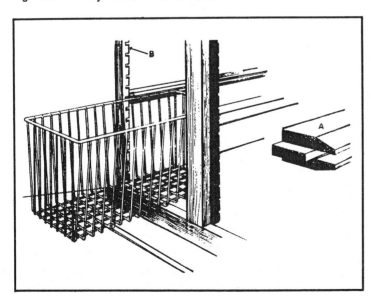

Fig. 2-36. A sliding basket for vegetables.

Concealed Sliding Garbage Pail

Garbage pails that pop out when you open the door of a base cabinet and disappear when the door is closed are really very handy. Unfortunately, the required mechanism is hard to get since it is usually sold only to professional kitchen dealers. You can, however, make a very simple kind of your own (Fig. 2-37). First, buy a tall plastic pail with a rolled lip around the top. A rectangular shape, as shown in the drawing, is best because it holds more than a round one. Make a frame of 3/4-inch lumber 3 inches wide, and nail and glue it together. The top (A) is made of 1/2-inch plywood with a cutout that permits the pail to drop in and hang by its overlapping lip. Side cutouts (B) allow your hands to get under the lip of the pail. The sides (C) are grooved to receive 1/2- × -1/2-inch drawer guides.

Sliding Broom and Brush Closet

Maybe *closet* isn't exactly the right name for this idea and perhaps *pull-out brush rack* is more accurate (Fig. 2-38). It should be located at the end of a counter and reach from the floor to the top of your wall cabinets. The rack consists of a narrow rectangular box frame of 3/4-inch plywood 6 inches wide. The vertical in front (A) is longer than the one in the back to conceal the top and bottom rollers. The edges of the frame on one side or the other should be rabbeted to receive a pegboard back (C) on which brooms, brushes, dust pans, etc.

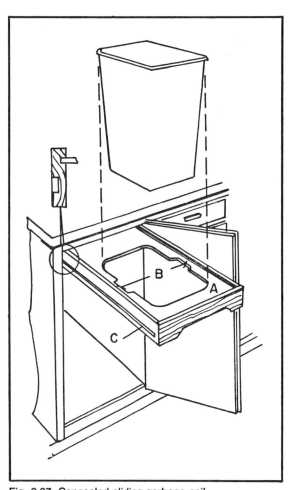

Fig. 2-37. Concealed sliding garbage pail.

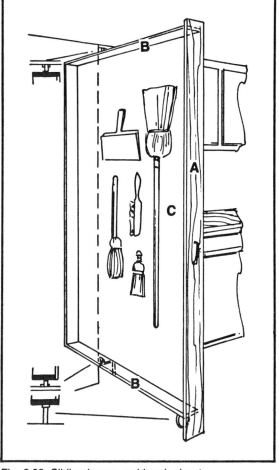

Fig. 2-38. Sliding broom and brush closet.

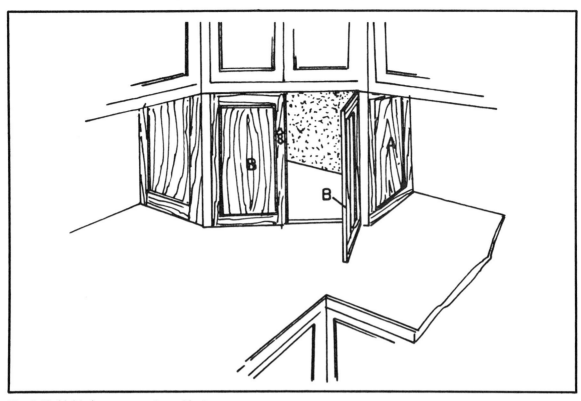

Fig. 2-39. Lighted corner counter cabinet.

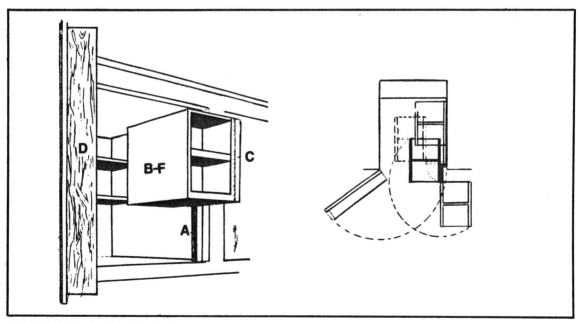

Fig. 2-40. Cabinet with swing shelves.

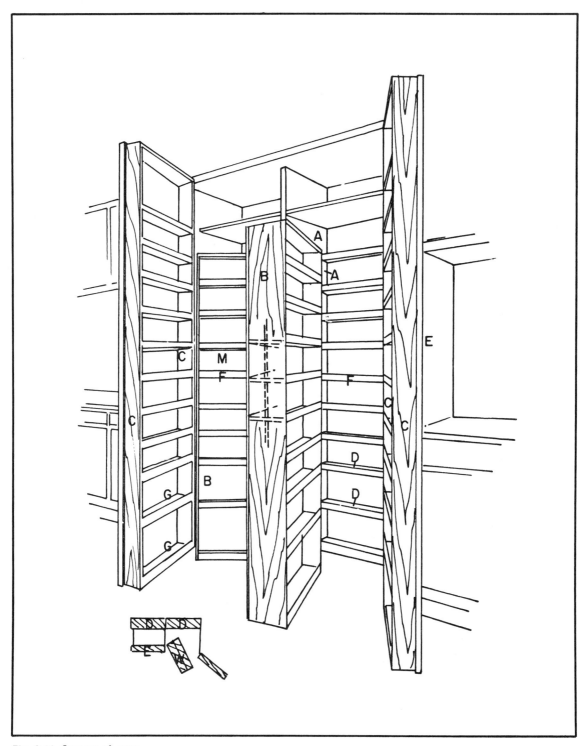

Fig. 2-41. Storage of cans.

can be hung on hooks. A plate-type, nonswiveling caster on the top horizontal (B) rides between two strips of wood nailed to the underside of the cabinet top. A similar caster rides on the cabinet floor between strips, and a larger caster rides on the kitchen floor.

Lighted Corner Counter Cabinet

If you have a catty-corner type of wall cabinet above the corner of an L-shaped counter, you can enclose the space below this cabinet as shown in Fig. 2-39 to conceal a mixer or toaster. The two sides (A) can be secured inside with angle irons and screws, and

the two doors (B) are hinged to the sides. The inside light is the ordinary closet door type, and magnetic catches hold the doors.

Cabinet with Swing Shelves

Two sets of shelves swing out of this cabinet (Fig. 2-40); one is on the inside of the door (D), and the other (B,F) is attached to the right interior side of the cabinet. The second set (B,F) is a stack of small shelves like boxes back to back attached by a hinge board (C), with two continuous hinges to a post (A). The drawing shows how the small shelves move as they swing out.

Fig. 2-42. Island Kitchen Cabinet.

Storage of Cans

Here's a pantry idea for maximum use of storage space (Fig. 2-41). The two swinging doors (E) are made of 3/4-inch plywood veneered on the outside to match other cabinets and are anchored to the sides of the pantry with full-length continuous hinges. The shelves (F) on the insides of the doors are 1/2-inch plywood dadoed into the sides (C) and backs (E) of the doors. The two inner swing shelf sections (W) have 1/2-inch shelves on both sides of a center partition (H) which is made of 3/4-inch

plywood. The sides of the swing sections (B) are made of 3/4-inch plywood 8 inches wide and are attached to the main partition (A) with full-length continuous hinges as shown in the diagram. The main partition should not be less than 1 1/2 inches thick. This thickness can be obtained by gluing two 3/4-inch sheets of plywood together and using screws for additional strength. The lip on the edge of each shelf (F) is simply a strip of 1/4-inch hardboard or plywood 1 inch high nailed into place. The space above the top shelf (J) is for storing large

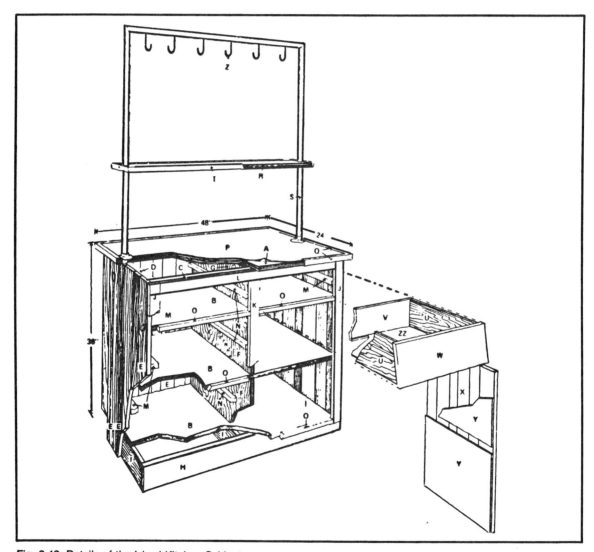

Fig. 2-43. Details of the Island Kitchen Cabinet.

Table 2-5. Materials for the Island Kitchen Cabinet.

A.	1 pc., 24″ × 48″ × 3/4″	S.	10 ft. of 1″ galvanized iron pipe
B.	3 pcs., 20 1/2″ × 44 1/2″ × 3/4″	T.	9 ft. of 1″ edge molding
C.	2 pcs., 1 1/2″ × 1 1/2″ × 44 1/2″ (1 pc. not shown)	U.	4 pcs., 5 1/2″ × 20 1/8″ × 3/8″ (2 pcs. not shown)
D.	2 pcs., 1 1/2″ × 1 1/2″ × 17 1/2″ (1 pc. not shown)	V.	2 pcs., 5 1/2″ × 19″ × 3/8″ (1 pc. not shown)
E.	random width boards, 31 3/4″ × 3/4″	W.	2 pcs., 6″ × 3/4″ × 20″ (1 pc. not shown)
F.	2 pcs., 11″ × 20 1/2″ × 3/4″	X.	random width boards, 22 3/4″ × 20″ × 3/4″
G.	1 pc., 7 1/2″ × 20 1/2″ × 3/4″	Y.	2 pcs., 20″ × 10 7/8″ × 1/4″
H.	2 pcs., 3 1/2″ × 3/4″ × 44 1/2″ (1 pc. not shown)	Z.	36 in. of 5/32″ wire bent to hooks
I.	3 pcs., 3 1/2″ × 3/4″ × 19″ (1 pc. not shown)	EE.	random width boards, 35 1/4″ × 3/4″
J.	2 pcs., 2″ × 3/4″ × 31 3/4″	NN.	8 pcs., 1/2″ × 3/4″ × 19 1/2″ (7 pcs. not shown)
K.	1 pc., 2″ × 3/4″ × 29 3/4″	ZZ.	4 pcs., 20 1/2″ × 18 5/8″ × 1/4″
L.	1 pc., 2″ × 3/4″ × 42″		
M.	4 pcs., 1″ × 1 1/2″ × 20 1/2″		Not shown: 2 large drawers
N.	4 pcs., 1″ × 7/8″ × 20 1/2″		
O.	5 pcs., 3/4″ × 3/4″ × 20″ (1pc. not shown)	UU.	4 sides, 11″ × 20 1/8″ × 3/8″
P.	formica top, 24″ × 48″	VV.	2 backs, 11″ × 20″ × 3/8″
Q.	12 ft. of metal edging	WW.	2 fronts, 11 1/2″ × 3/4″ × 20″
R.	1 pc., 6″ × 48″ × 3/4″		

packages. There are two rows of narrow 4- to 5-inch shelves (D), one on each side of the main partition (A), which are attached to the back wall of the pantry, the partition, and one pantry side.

SAVE STEPS WITH AN ISLAND KITCHEN CABINET

If you are fortunate enough to have a large kitchen, you will find an island cabinet very useful. Not only does it provide convenient storage space and a large work surface, but it also saves a great deal of walking back and forth because of its central location.

Although this cabinet (Fig. 2-42) is made of random-width boards to match the style of the original cabinets in the room, it can easily be made out of plywood with a few modifications to match your own kitchen cabinets.

The iron pipework frame is easier to make than it looks. You can cut the pipe with a hacksaw, and the mitered joints can be put together for you by a professional welder. The hooks are made of 1/4-inch soft steel rod bent into shape and welded or brazed into holes previously drilled. The little spice shelf under the pots has a molding around it that sticks up just high enough to prevent the spice cans from falling off. The ends of the shelf are secured by a screw that goes through holes drilled into the shelf ends.

Refer to Fig. 2-43 and Table 2-5. Note that the door on the right side has random-width boards (X) fastened together with glue and screws to two sheets of 1/4-inch plywood or hardboard (Y). The guides on the drawers (NN) should be located so that they ride on guides in the cabinet (M and N). When you are cutting the sides of the drawers, remember to cut the front edges at an angle so that the drawer fronts slant as shown in Fig. 2-42. Also note that while the random-width boards (E) around the back and ends are 33 3/4 inches long, those that extend to the floor on both ends (EE) are 35 1/4 inches.

The edging around the laminated plastic top is stainless steel and is available in larger hardware stores. It is best to bend this edging around the corners rather than cut it into four separate strips. Bending is very easy once you have notched the edging for mitered corners.

Chapter 3

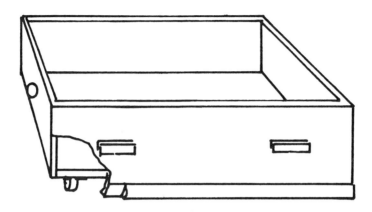

Bedroom Projects

Do your children need to double-up in bedrooms? Do you have enough room for everyone? Once you've built some of the projects in this chapter, you'll have no more complaints. Not only are there projects to increase space, but some, like the platform for a teenager's room and the desk for a boy's room, will also bring pleasing compliments from your family.

CONSTRUCT A DESK
AND STORAGE CABINET COMBO

If you've got two boys in a room, you'll find the project in Fig. 3-1 a very satisfying way of providing ample storage space for their clothing, toys, and athletic equipment, as well as splendid desks for schoolwork.

The desk tops are extremely easy to make and call for no special skill. See Fig. 3-2 and Table 3-1. The tops (C) consist of the two halves of a standard, hollow, birch veneer door cut down its length with a saw. Each half is laid on top of a pair of cabinets (B and H,D), as shown in Fig. 3-2. The desk tops

are fastened to the cabinets by screws driven through the undersides of the cabinet tops into the framework of the hollow door (C).

You may need to insert some wood blocks between the veneered sheets of the door halves along the edges that touch the wall to stiffen the surface at these points because there is no framing left along these back edges. If you find this necessary, fasten the blocks in place with glue and clamps instead of nails, to avoid marring the surface of the top.

The two center cabinets (B) are unfinished furniture purchased at a department store. They are also available from mail-order houses and stores which specialize in unfinished furniture. The overhang of the tops of these two cabinets are cut flush with the sides and fronts. Both cabinets are screwed to each other through the two sides that butt together.

The cabinets at the far ends are made of 3/4-inch plywood with the tops and bottoms rabbeted to the sides and fastened with nails and glue. The sliding doors (H) of these cabinets are made

Fig. 3-1. Desk and Storage Cabinet Combo.

of tempered, perforated hardboard. They slide in grooves (Cabinet Detail) cut into the tops, bottoms, and sides. The doors must be slipped into their grooves when the cabinet is assembled.

The two wall cabinets, like the two end cabinets below them, have no backs. They are assembled with rabbet joints and fastened with nails and glue. Both wall cabinets are nailed to cleats (I,J), which are screwed to wall studs. The upper cleat (I) is inside the cabinets. The center partition (L) is nailed through the top and bottom. Both sliding doors (M) are made of perforated hardboard and slide in tracks, as shown in the Cabinet Detail.

SAVE SPACE WITH
A CLOSET BUNK COMBINATION

The bunk bedcloset combination is a very handy

arrangement for the family that has two boys in a bedroom. This particular design will work well also for one boy with room for a guest (Fig. 3-3). The lower bunk can be used either for sleeping or as a couch for sitting.

The upper bunk is supported by the closet and by lag screws driven through the side (A) of the bunk against the wall into the studs (Table 3-2 and Fig. 3-4). The foot of the bunk (C) is also fastened to the wall in the same manner as A. Two long bolts can be used to fasten the bottom (F) of the bunk to the top of the cabinet (G), although it may not be strictly necessary.

The closet is simply a box made of 3/4-inch plywood with a back (L) of 1/2-inch hardboard. Make the floor of 3/4-inch plywood and use finishing nails driven through the front (K), sides (H), and back (L) to fasten it into place. Use both

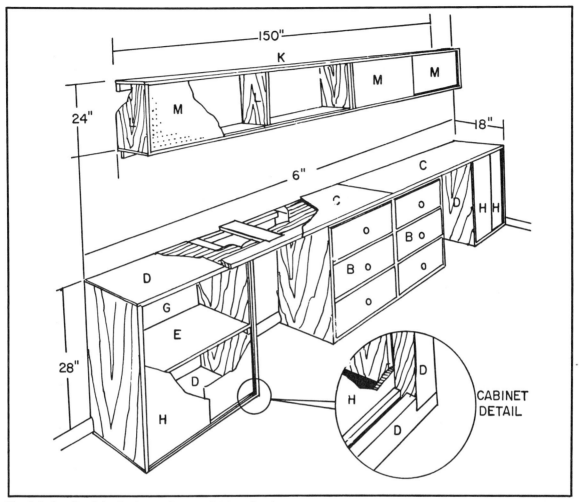

Fig. 3-2. Details of the Desk and Storage Cabinet Combo.

Table 3-1. Materials for the Desk and Storage Cabinet Combo.

A.	2 pcs, each: 79″ × 2″ × 1″ (1 not shown)
B.	2 chests of drawers, each: 28″ × 28″ × 18″
C.	1 standard hollow birch veneer door, 81″ × 36″ × 1″
D.	8 pcs, each: 28″ × 18″ × 1″ (1 not shown)
E.	2 pcs, each: 26″ × 16″ × 3/4″ (1 not shown)
F.	4 pcs, each: 16″ × 2″ × 1″ (3 not shown)
G.	2 pcs, each: 28″ × 28″ × 1/8″ (1 not shown)
H.	4 pcs, each: 26″ × 15″ × 1/8″
I.	2 pcs, each: 73″ × 2″ × 1″ (1 not shown)
J.	2 pcs, each: 75″ × 2″ × 1″ (1 not shown)
K.	4 pcs, each: 75″ × 12″ × 1″
L.	6 pcs, each: 24″ × 12″ × 1″
M.	4 pcs, each: 38 1/2″ × 22″ × 1/8″ (1 not shown)

Fig. 3-3. Closet/Bunk Combination.

Table 3-2. Materials for the Closet/Bunk Combination.

A.	2 pcs, 3/4" × 11 1/4" × 75 3/4"	O.	3 pcs, 3/4" × 15 3/4" × 28 3/4"
B.	1 pc, 3/4" × 11 1/4" × 31 1/2"	P.	1 pc, 1/2" × 15 3/4" × 75"
C.	1 pc, 3/4" × 4" × 30"	Q.	1 pc, 1/4" × 1 1/4" × 30"
		R.	1 pc, 1/4" × 1 1/4" × 75 1/4"
D.	2 pcs, 3/4" × 3/4" × 75"	S.	1 pc, 3/4" × 15 3/4" × 75"
E.	2 pcs, 3/4" × 3/4" × 28 1/2"	T.	1 pc, 3/4" × 1 1/2" × 8"
F.	2 pcs, 3/4" × 30" × 75"	U.	8 pcs, 1 1/2" thick triangles
G.	2 pcs, 3/4" × 29 1/2" × 43 1/2"	V.	1 pc, 3/4" × 8" × 42"
H.	2 pcs, 3/4" × 30 3/4" × 56"	W.	1 pc, 1/2" × 7 1/2" × 39 1/2"
I.	2 pcs, 3/4" × 1 1/2" × 49 1/2"	X.	1 pc, 3/4" × 2" × 28 3/4"
J.	1 pc, 1 1/2" × 1 1/2" × 45"	Y.	1 pcs, 1/2" × 28 3/4" × 40 1/2"
K.	1 pc, 1 1/2" × 5" × 45"	Z.	2 pcs, 1/2" × 7 1/2" × 28 3/4"
L.	1 pc, 1/2" × 43 1/2" × 56"	AA.	2 pcs, 3/4" × 3 1/2" × 70"
M.	2 pcs, 1/2" × 21 1/2" × 50"	BB.	4 pcs, 3/4" × 3 1/2" × 20"
N.	6 pcs, 3/4" × 3/4" × 28 3/4"	CC.	2 pcs, 3/4" × 3/4" × 43 1/2"

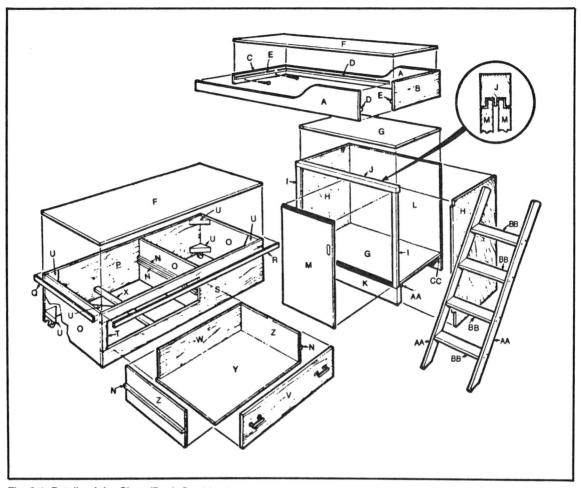

Fig. 3-4. Details of the Closet/Bunk Combination.

glue and nails for all joints. Nail heads should be countersunk and puttied.

The sliding doors of the closet are made of 1/2-inch plywood rabbeted top and bottom to provide an edge which is 1/4-inch thick and rides on rollers of the type used in medicine cabinets for sliding glass mirror doors. If you have trouble obtaining these rollers, use the standard plastic or aluminum tracks with grooves for 1/4-inch material. They are available in many hardware stores. You can eliminate rollers and tracks by simply cutting smooth 1/4-inch grooves in the top and bottom of the front (K,J) and waxing them. note the arrangement shown in Fig. 3-4 for guiding the doors at the top.

The bottom bunk is quite different from the upper one. Basically it is a box with 3/4-inch ends (O) and 1/2-inch plywood back. The right front side (covered by the closet) is covered by a solid sheet of plywood. The left side has a deep drawer (V) for storage. Note the 2 × 2 (X) that runs from the lower left front of S to the back, which serves not only as a brace for the bunk at this point but also provides a (waxed) rail on which the bottom of the drawer can slide. Of course, the drawer also has side guides.

Note the triangular braces (U) in each corner to which casters are attached so that the bunk can be pulled out of its recess to be made up when desired. The ladder can be made any style you choose and is, of course, light and movable.

A paint finish is best for this project. Two coats of primer with light sanding between coats and a finish coat of the desired color should do the job.

BUILD INTO A LITTLE GIRL'S ROOM

This built-in bunk, storage drawer, shelves, and desk for a small girl's room (Fig. 3-5) is an attractive combination. Refer to Figs. 3-6 and 3-7. The two bookshelves are made of 3/4-inch plywood with shelves that are glued and nailed through the sides (Table 3-3).

To avoid making the shelves too deep, cleats (B) are nailed to the inner surfaces of the sides. The 1/4-inch plywood that forms the back of the shelves is nailed to these cleats, as well as the back of each shelf. A 1-×-4 facing (A) provides additional reinforcement at the top in front.

The 1/2-inch plywood sheet (C) that supports the 4-inch-thick foam mattress of the bunk bed rests on cleats (E,H), which are nailed to the studs of the back wall and to the inner sides of the bookshelves (I). A brace (G) half-lapped to the side cleats (E) helps prevent any possible sagging of the plywood sheet (C), which is nailed and glued to the cleats.

To strengthen the front edge of the bed on which an adult might sit, the 1-×-4 facing (D) is reinforced by a long, steel angle iron which runs along the full length of the facing on the inner side and is screwed to it. A pair of 2-inch angle irons supports the ends of the long angle iron (F) and are screwed to the sides of the bookshelves (I) and

Fig. 3-5. Built-in Bunk, Storage Drawers, Shelves, and Desk for a Little Girl's Room.

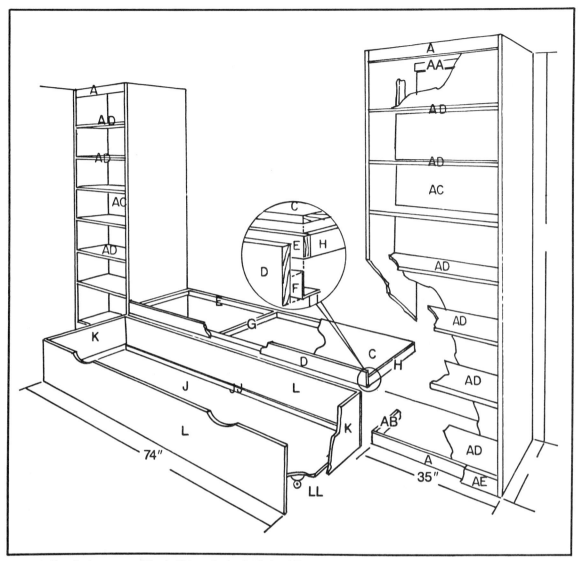

Fig. 3-6. Details for some of the built-in units in the little girl's room.

bolted to the long angle iron as shown in Fig. 3-6. The inner side of the front facing (D) is recessed to receive its angle iron reinforcement.

The bunk bed should provide a 1-inch space all around the mattress to permit you to tuck in blankets and sheets without cramping your fingers. The storage drawer may be used as a second bed if you have two children in this room. The second bed is simply a large box made of 3/4-inch plywood. It is glued and nailed with butt joints.

The 3/4-inch plywood sheet (J) that supports the mattress is attached to the sides (L) and ends (K) with nails and glue. The exact location of this plywood sheet inside the box depends on the thickness of the mattress, which should come no higher than 1/2-inch below the tops of the sides and ends.

Four casters with 1 1/2 inch soft rubber tires attached to the bottom of the plywood sheet (J) will permit the bed to be moved in and out with the

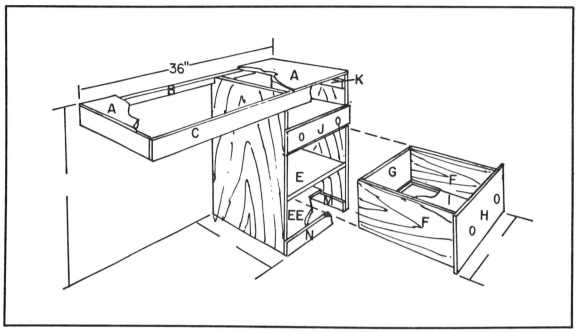

Fig. 3-7. Details of the desk for the little girl's room.

greatest of ease. If the bottom of the plywood sheet is too high to reach the tops of the casters, use wooden blocks screwed and glued to the underside of the sheet to make up the difference. The caster wheels should protrude at least 1/4 inch below the bottom edges of the sides. The casters should be located about 12 inches in from the ends.

The little girl's desk, seen in front of the win-dow, is modernistic and unusual, yet eminently practical. The open left side without any legs or supports permits a child to swing her legs in or out under the desk with ease and comfort.

The desk top (A) is nailed to a cleat (B), which is fastened to the wall with screws and also nailed to the apron supports D and C (Table 3-4). The butt-joint outer corners (B-D, C-D) are reinforced on the

Table 3-3. Materials for the Bookshelves and Bunk in the Little Girl's Room.

BED				
A.	4 pcs, each: 34 1/2″ × 4″ × 1″		AA.	2 pcs, each: 34 1/2″ × 2″ × 2″
B.	4 pcs, each: 96″ × 2″ × 1″		AB.	4 pcs, each: 31″ × 3″ × 1″
C.	1 pc, 74″ × 31″ × 1/2″		AC.	2 pcs, each: 96″ × 34″ × 1/4″
D.	1 pc, 74″ × 4″ × 1″		AD.	14 pcs, each: 34 1/2″ × 12″ × 1″
E.	1 pc, 74″ × 2″ × 1″		AE.	2 pcs, each: 34 1/2″ × 5″ × 1″
F.	1 steel angle iron, 74″ × 2″ × 2″		FF.	2 angle irons, each: 2″ × 2″ × 1″
G.	1 pc, 30 3/4″ × 2″ × 2″		JJ.	2 pcs, each: 72 1/2″ × 2″ × 1″
H.	2 pcs, each: 29 3/4″ × 2″ × 1″		KK.	2 pcs, each: 28 1/2″ × 2″ × 1″
I.	4 pcs, each: 96″ × 32″ × 3/4″		LL.	4 casters with 1 1/2″ soft rubber
J.	1 pc, 72 1/2″ × 30 1/2″ × 3/4″			tires
K.	2 pcs, each: 30 1/2″ × 14″ × 3/4″			
L.	2 pcs, each: 74″ × 14″ × 3/4″			

Table 3-4. Materials for the Desk in the Little Girl's Room.

DESK		J.	2 drawers, each:
A.	1 pc, 36″ × 18″ × 1″		1 front, 14″ × 2 15/16″ × 3/4″;
B.	1 pc, 34″ × 2″ × 2″		2 sides, 17 3/16″ × 2 3/16″ × 1/2″;
C.	1 pc, 36″ × 3″ × 1″		1 back, 11 7/8″ × 2 3/16″ × 1/2″;
D.	1 pc, 17″ × 3″ × 1″		1 bottom, 16 15/16″ × 12″ × 1/4″
E.	3 pcs, each: 17″ × 12″ × 1″	K.	2 pcs, each: 17″ × 2″ × 1″
F.	4 pcs, each: 17 3/16″ × 5 3/16″ × 1/2″	L.	2 pcs, each: 25″ × 17″ × 1″
		M.	2 pcs, each: 17″ × 3″ × 1″
G.	2 pcs, each: 11 7/8″ × 5 3/16″ × 1/2″	N.	1 pc, 14″ × 4″ × 1″
H.	2 pcs, each: 14″ × 4 15/16″ × 3/4″	EE.	1 pc, 17″ × 12″ × 1″
I.	2 pcs, each: 16 15/16″ × 12″ × 1/4″		

insides with 2-inch angle irons. The wall cleat (B) and front apron (C) are nailed and glued to the sides (L) of the drawer cabinet. The shelves on which the drawers slide (E) are fastened in place with finishing nails driven through the sides (L). However, the bottom shelf (EE) rests on two side cleats (M), as well as one in the back against the wall.

Note that the drawer fronts (H,J) overlap the edges of the sides (L), and that their ends are flush with the sides. The drawer fronts are also closely fitted to each other above and below and are flush with each other.

The drawers are very simply made out of 1/2-inch plywood (F,F,G) with glued and nailed butt joints. The drawer fronts (H,J) are made of 3/4-inch lumber and, like the sides and back (G) are grooved to receive the 1/4-inch plywood bottom (I).

The decorative aspects depend on your own taste. Use a good grade of semigloss interior enamel for the desk, beds, and shelves. Brush or spray it on.

STORE SMALL ITEMS

Children always have all sorts of small toys and junk that they love to scatter around the room. Here's a marvelously simple and inexpensive way to keep all of these small items gathered.

The shelves seen in Fig. 3-8 are simply 3/4-inch boards of clear pine 14 inches wide and about 5 feet long (Table 3-5). (The length depends on the space you have available.) The "drawers" are plastic con-

tainers easily obtained in any home furnishings store. Make the L-shaped drawer guides as shown in Fig. 3-9 using 1 3/4-inch screws that go through the guides into the underside of the shelves. Twelve-inch brackets support the shelves. Screws in these brackets are driven into studs behind the wall. Finish the shelves in a good grade of enamel.

BUILD A HIDEAWAY BED COMBO

Ever try to shoehorn a teenager and a younger child into the same room? You could with this hideaway bed combo (Fig. 3-10) and have room to spare. Not only does this project provide both a measure of privacy, but the beds fold up when not in use.

The utility of this project is increased by the large amounts of storage space it provides both above and below the beds. The room divider doubles as a hideaway for two fullsize beds. The novel way the beds are supported does away with the need for fixed supports.

Refer to Fig. 3-11 and Table 3-6. The entire project can be made from pine. As is usual in projects of this type, the fixed portions of it should be built first, with movable portions such as the bed (S,T) and its supports (R) built last. There are bullet-stop catches (AE) imbedded in the edge of the bed (S) that serve as a bed stop.

Most pieces of the project can be joined together using simple butt joints, nails, and glue. One of the exceptions is the bookcase portion, most of whose shelves (L) are dadoed into the uprights (E),

Fig. 3-8. Storage for small items.

Table 3-5. Materials for the Small-Item Storage Project.

A.	2 pcs, 3/4″ × 14″ × 60″
B.	12 pcs, 3/4″ × 3/4″ × 12″
C.	12 pcs, 3/8″ × 1 1/4″ × 12″
D.	8 brackets, 10″ × 12″

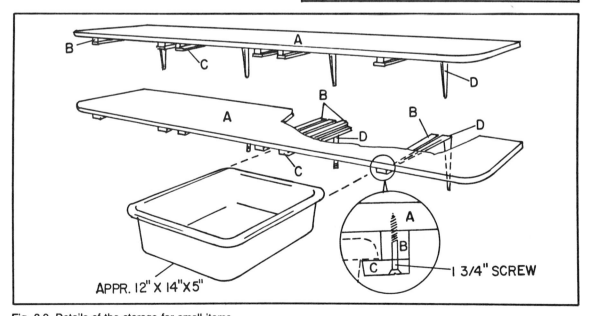

APPR. 12″ X 14″X 5″

1 3/4″ SCREW

Fig. 3-9. Details of the storage for small items.

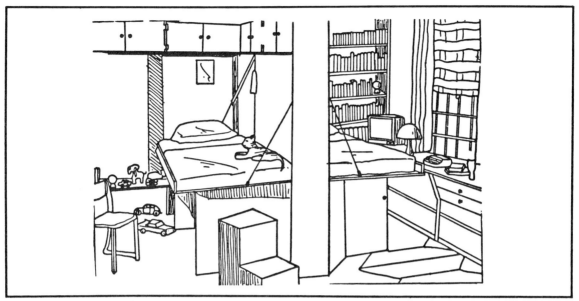

Fig. 3-10. Hideaway Bed Combo.

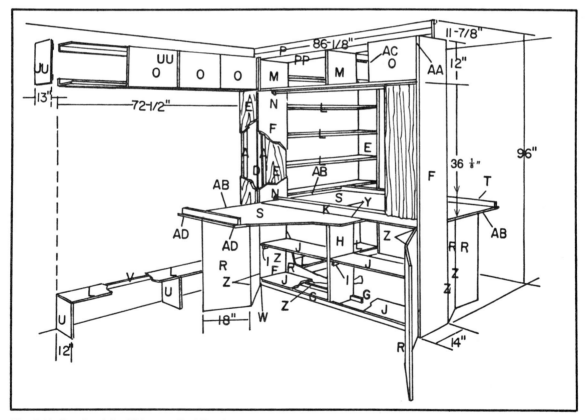

Fig. 3-11. Details of the Hideaway Bed Combo.

59

Table 3-6. Materials for the Hideaway Bed Combo.

A.	2 pcs, each: 84 1/8″ × 2″ × 1″	Q.	1 pc, 86 1/8″ × 1″ × 1″
B.	4 pcs, each: 8″ × 2″ × 1″ (not shown)	R.	8 pcs, each: 36″ × 18″ × 1″
		S.	2 pcs, each: 72″ × 36″ × 1″
C.	4 pcs, each: 9″ × 2″ × 1″ (not shown)	T.	2 pcs, each: 71″ × 3″ × 1″
		U.	3 pcs, each: 12″ × 12″ × 1″ (1 not shown)
D.	2 pcs, each: 84 1/8″ × 2″ × 2″		
E.	3 pcs, each: 84 1/8″ × 12″ × 1″	V.	3 pcs, each: 72 1/2″ × 2″ × 1″
F.	2 pcs, each: 84 1/8″ × 14″ × 1″	W.	4 angle irons, 2″ × 2″ (3 not shown)
G.	4 pcs, each: 72 1/2″ × 3″ × 1″ (1 not shown)		
		Y.	2 piano or continuous hinges, each: 71″
H.	1 pc, 36″ × 12″ × 1″		
I.	8 pcs, each: 10″ × 2″ × 1″ (6 not shown)	Z.	8 piano or continuous hinges, each: 35″
		AA.	24 hinges, each: 2″ × 1″ (8 not shown)
J.	4 pcs, each: 35 9/16″ × 12″ × 1″		
K.	1 pc, 72 1/2″ × 14″ × 1″	AB.	4 eye-bolts (1 not shown)
L.	12 pcs, each: 72 1/2″ × 12″ × 1″	AC.	16 door pulls (12 not shown)
M.	2 pcs, each: 14″ × 12″ × 1″	AD.	8 bullet-stop catches (6 not shown)
N.	2 curtain rods, each: 72 1/2″		
O.	12 doors, each: 18″ × 12″ × 1″ (8 not shown)	PP.	1 pc, 86 1/8″ × 12″ × 1″
P.	1 pc, 86 1/8″ × 11 7/8″ × 1″	UU.	2 pcs, each: 13″ × 12″ × 1″

also using the nails and glue. The overhead storage cabinets located in the upper portions of the room divider open from either side and use a different type of joint. Both its center and end boards (M) are notched in the middle to receive the cross pieces (L,PP). The center piece (H) of the storage space underneath the beds in notched on either side of its lower end to fit into the space between the two horizontal pieces (G).

When you start to build this project, you should first build a frame against the wall using items B and C as part of the horizontal framing elements at top and bottom and pieces A and D as the vertical elements of the frame. Pieces E and F are then used to cover the frame. Before installing the piece (E) that forms one side of the bookcase, it is a good idea to cut dadoes in it to receive the horizontal members (L).

Two of the uprights (F) are anchored to the floor using angle irons (W). Additional anchoring is obtained by securing Q to ceiling joists with screws and attaching PP to it.

PROVIDE A PLATFORM FOR A TEENAGER'S ROOM

A platform in a teenager's room can do wonders for its appearance (Fig. 3-12). If you need some extra storage space, and who doesn't, the space under the platform can be put to good use in the form of added drawers.

Construction of the platform can be vastly simplified if the drawers underneath it are considered as a row of boxes with open-end fronts. For some people, all the drawer space may not be necessary, in which case construction is simpler.

The "boxes" under the platform are made of 3/4-inch plywood and are screwed together through the sides with 1 1/4-inch screws (Fig. 3-13 and Table 3-7). The sides of the boxes joined together provide 1 1/2-inch supports for the platform and are stronger than the complicated framing that would otherwise have to be used.

The boxes have to be fastened together before the platform cover is laid down. The platform is

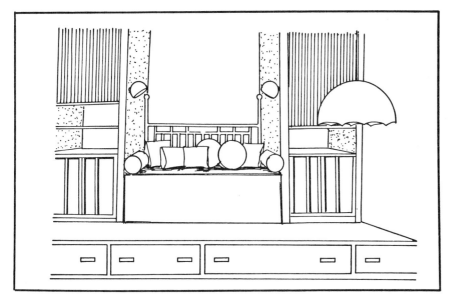

Fig. 3-12. Platform for
a Teenager's Room.

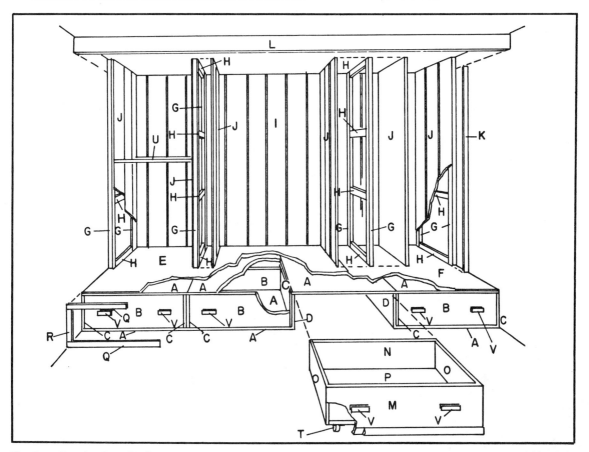

Fig. 3-13. Details of the Platform.

Table 3-7. Materials for the Platform.

A.	7 pcs, 3/4″ × 36″ × 48″	K.	4 pcs, 2″ × 77 3/4″ wall panel
B.	11 pcs, 3/4″ × 10 1/2″ × 34 1/2″	L.	1 pc, 1/2″ × 6″ × 144″
C.	6 pcs, 3/4″ × 10 1/2″ × 48″	M.	1 pc, 3/4″ × 11 1/8″ × 34 3/8″
D.	2 pcs, 3/4″ × 11 3/4″ × 48″	N.	1 pc, 3/4″ × 8″ × 32 7/8″
E.	1 pc, 1/4″ × 48″ × 96″ hardboard	O.	2 pcs, 3/4″ × 8″ × 24″
F.	1 pc, 1/4″ × 48″ × 48″	P.	1 pc, 3/4″ × 23 1/4″ × 23 7/8″
G.	8 pcs, 1 1/2″ × 2 1/2″ × 83 3/4″	Q.	1/4″ × 1 1/2″ trim
H.	16 pcs, 1 1/2″ × 2 1/2″ × 19″	R.	1/4″ × 1 1/2″ trim
I.	83 3/4″ × 144″ wall panel	S.	1/4″ × 1 1/2″ trim
J.	6 pcs, 83 3/4″ × 24″ wall panel	T.	4 pcs, casters
		U.	4 pcs, 3/4″ × 23 1/2″ × 33 1/4″
		V.	8 pcs, 3/4″ × 3/4″ × 4″

made of 3/4-inch plywood sheets joined to the tops of the box sides with screws and glue. Since the plywood is not visible anywhere except for the fronts of the drawers, you can use the rough construction type.

The partitions on either side of the bed-couch are made of 2 × 3s covered with wall paneling. The space above the furniture cabinets has adjustable shelves. They can be concealed by the bright window shades which act as pull-down "doors".

MAKE A DESK FOR A BOY'S ROOM

Figure 3-14 shows a boy's room in a refinished at-

Fig. 3-14. Desk for a Boy's Room.

tic with an extremely practical desk that is easy to make, provides plenty of storage, and has ample work space on the top surface.

Refer to Fig. 3-15 and Table 3-8. The top (A) is a sheet of 3/4-inch plywood with a 1 3/4-inch skirt of 1/2-inch-thick lumber fastened with finishing nails and glue. The left end of the desk top is supported by a cleat attached with screws driven through the plasterboard and into the studs.

The right end of the desk top is supported by a cabinet which is really a three-sided box made up of the back and two sides (D) nailed to a top and bottom (J). The top of this box (J) is attached to the underside of the desk top (A) with glue and 1 1/4-inch No. 8 screws. The door of the cabinet is equipped with a touch latch and therefore needs no exterior handle.

The decorative frames (E, F, I, L, K and H, G, H, G) on the surfaces of the door, sides, and back of the cabinet are made of 1/2-inch lumber with routed edges. If you are not equipped to do this kind of routing, just round off the corners and smooth them with sandpaper. The frames are fastened with countersunk finishing nails and glue. The nail holes are filled with wood putty. Note that the cabinet door has a 1/8-inch clearance at the bottom so that it can swing freely over the floor.

The plywood for the desk top should be good

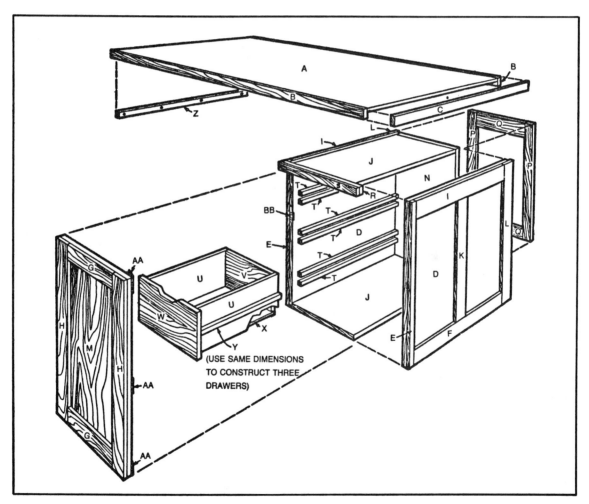

Fig. 3-15. Details of the Boy's Desk.

Table 3-8. Materials for the Desk for a Boy's Room.

A.	1 pc, 3/4″ × 22 1/2″ × 59 1/4″
B.	2 pcs, 3/4″ × 1 3/4″ × 59 1/4″
C.	1 pc, 3/4″ × 1 3/4″ × 24″
D.	2 pcs, 3/4″ × 20 3/4″ × 28 1/4″
E.	2 pcs, 1/2″ × 3/4″ × 28 1/4″
F.	2 pcs, 1/2″ × 2″ × 18 1/2″
G.	2 pcs, 1/2″ × 2″ × 10 1/2″
H.	2 pcs, 1/2″ × 2″ × 28″
I.	2 pcs, 1/2″ × 3 1/2″ × 18 1/2″
J.	2 pcs, 3/4″ × 12″ × 20″
K.	2 pcs, 1/2″ × 2″ × 23″
L.	2 pcs, 1/2″ × 2″ × 28 1/4″
M.	1 pc, 3/4″ × 14 1/2″ × 28″
N.	1 pc, 3/4″ × 12″ × 28 1/4″
O.	1 pc, 1/2″ × 3 1/4″ × 10 1/2″
P.	2 pcs, 1/2″ × 1 1/2″ × 28 1/4″
Q.	1 pc, 1/2″ × 2″ × 10 1/2″
R.	1 pc, 3/4″ × 1 1/4″ × 14 1/2″
S.	1 pc, 1/2″ × 1 1/4″ × 14 1/2″
T.	12 pcs, 3/4″ × 3/4″ × 18 3/4″
U.	6 pcs, 1/2″ × 6 5/8″ × 16″
V.	3 pcs, 1/2″ × 6 5/8″ × 9 1/4″
W.	3 pcs, 3/4″ × 6 5/8″ × 11 3/4″
X.	3 pcs, 1/4″ × 9 3/4″ × 15 3/4″
Y.	6 pcs, 3/4″ × 3/4″ × 16″
Z.	1 pc, 3/4″ × 1″ × 22 1/2″
AA.	3 pcs, hinges
BB.	1 pc, magnetic latch

one side and sanded when purchased. It should then be sanded again with 100-grit and then with 150-grit aluminum oxide open coat sandpaper. Follow with two, or even three, coats of fresh shellac diluted half and half with alcohol. Each coat of shellac should be rubbed smooth with fine steel wool. Spray with a wood primer followed by two coats of the enamel color of your choice. Rub both coats of enamel lightly with very fine steel wool and then apply a good grade of paste wax.

MATCH WALL PANELING ON FURNITURE

Adding prefinished hardwood paneling to your little girl's room as an oversized valance with matching bed frame, benches, and canopy can make it look like something your little girl might have dreamed of. See Fig. 3-16.

This dream is easy to make come true at a cost far lower than you'd think, using only a saber saw, hammer, and the materials listed in Table 3-9. The suggested method of cutting the 4-×-8 hardwood panels indicated in Details 6, 7, 8, and 9 of Fig. 3-17 takes maximum advantage of the beautiful grain which runs parallel to the longest dimension of a 4-×-8-foot panel with minimum waste.

A nice feature wives will appreciate is that both end piece T (joined to sides D with catches S) and the sides (resting loosely against the side benches) can be easily removed and replaced for cleaning

under and around the 72-×-36-inch bed.

The valances (H) are located 6 inches from the wall on all sides to allow the installation of fluorescent lamps on the ceiling if desired. Pieces A, B, G, and GG are attached to the ceiling joists with nails or screws. Pieces GG (1-×-2 strips not included in Table 3-8) are shown merely so you can see how the valances are continued around the ceiling of the room. Detail 4 of Fig. 3-17 shows the patterns for making curved cuts in the paneling. All paneling, including that of the canopy, is attached to their 1-×-2 braces using 1-inch finishing nails and glue.

Piece M is attached to piece L using either contact cement or regular panel adhesive. Detail 1 of Fig. 3-17 shows a glue block (I) installed; Detail 2 shows glue block (E); Detail 3 shows the construction of the side benches—not meant to be sat on—in which piece J is first attached directly to the wall studs with either nails or screws.

Painting or finishing this project should present no problem. The prefinished hardwood paneling is easily cleaned, and its surface is already beautifully decorative.

BUILD SHIPSHAPE STORAGE FOR A BOY'S ROOM

For your boy's room, here's an easily constructed

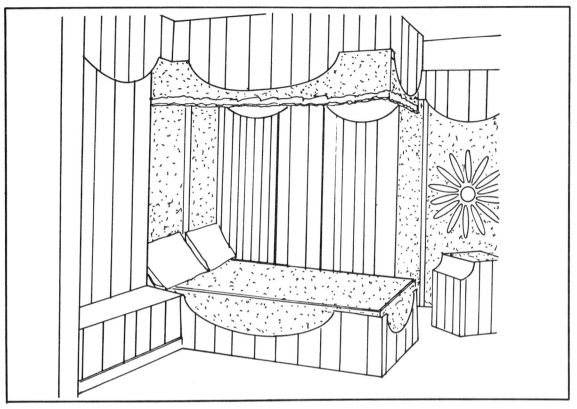

Fig. 3-16. Wall paneling matched on furniture in a little girl's room.

Table 3-9. Materials for the Valance, Bed Frame, Benches, and Canopy.

A. 2 pcs, each: 75″ × 1 1/2″ × 1 1/2″
B. 1 pc, 40″ × 1 1/2″ × 1 1/2″
C. 4 pcs, each: 37 1/2″ × 26 1/2″ × 3/4″ (see pattern)
D. 4 pcs, each: 37 1/2″ × 20″ × 1/4″ (see pattern)
E. 6 pcs, each: 6″ × 3/4″ × 3/4″ (3 not shown)
F. 1 pc, 43 1/2″ × 26 1/2″ × 1/4″ (see pattern)
G. 2 pcs, each: 43″ × 1 1/2″ × 11/2″
H. 2 pcs, (at least), each: 43″ × 26 1/2″ × 1/4″ (see pattern, exact number is determined by size of room)
I. 2 pcs, each: 6″ × 3/4″ × 3/4″ (1 not shown)
J. 2 pcs, each: 48 1/2″ × 1 1/2″ × 1 1/2″ (1 not shown)

K. 8 pcs, each: 13 1/2″ × 1 1/2″ × 1 1/2″ (5 not shown)
L. 2 pcs, each: 51 1/2″ × 17 3/4″ × 1 1/2″ (1 not shown)
M. 2 pcs, each: 51 1/2″ × 17 3/4″
N. 2 pcs, each: 48 1/2″ × 11 3/4″ × 1/2″ (1 not shown)
O. 2 pcs, each: 51 1/2″ × 14″ × 1/4″
P. 2 pcs, each: 72 3/4″ × 1 1/2″ × 3/4″ (1 not shown)
Q. 2 pcs, each: 6″ × 1 1/2″ × 3/4″ (1 not shown)
R. 4 pcs, each: 18″ × 1 1/2″ × 3/4″
S. catches
T. 1 pc, 43 1/2″ × 20″ × 1/4″ (see pattern)
CC. 2 pcs, each: 24″ × 1 1/2″ × 3/4″ (1 not shown)

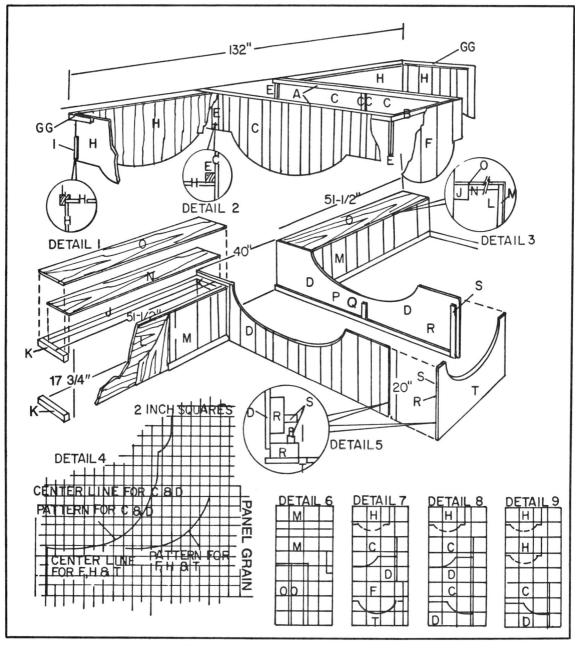

Fig. 3-17. Details of the valance, bed frame, benches, and canopy for the little girl's room.

plywood unit that features a convenient seat, a bookcase, and storage areas. There is plenty of much-needed storage space in the large under-the-seat drawer, side laundry bin, hide-away drop-leaf

storage bin (hidden behind the back cushion in Fig. 3-18), compartment with sliding doors, and ceiling storage compartment. Although Fig. 3-18 shows a nautical motif, the project, of course, will lend itself

Fig. 3-18. Shipshape Storage for a Boy's Room.

to whatever decorating theme you choose.

Refer to Fig. 3-19 and Table 3-10. The side panels (A) of the 8-foot high storage/shelf section are nailed directly to the wall, which is later painted to harmonize with the color of the rest of the unit. Note that the frontal area (D) of the top compartment is enclosed for decorating purposes. The hollow area behind the front panel (D) is not wasted, however. Access is from a small, inconspicuous door (FF) on the side. This area is perfect for long-term storage of long, thin items such as fishing poles and baseball bats. The shelves (B) are nailed to the side panels (A) and further supported by decorative molding (G). The lower shelf area is enclosed with sliding doors (GG) fitted into grooves cut in the lower shelf (B). The front panel (F) of the bottom section—later completely hidden by the seat, seat cushions, and storage bin—has a drop leaf (R) cut from it. The drop leaf is hinged and has a finger hole and drop chain for convenient opening. Blocks (DD) under lower shelf (B) with magnetic catches are included for closing the drop leaf.

The front and back panels (H) of the seat and side storage bin part of the unit are 32- x -54-inch panels with an 18- x -30-inch section cut from them to form an L shape. Appropriately sized sections from the front panel (H) are cut to accommodate the drawer and laundry bin. Side panels (I,J) are

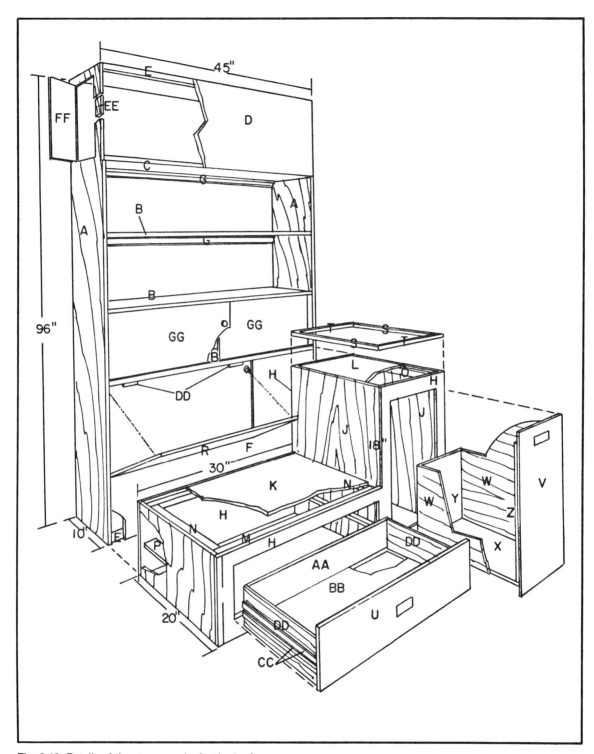

Fig. 3-19. Details of the storage units for the boy's room.

Table 3-10. Materials for the Seat, Bookcase, and Storage Areas.

A.	2 pcs., 3/4" × 10" × 96"		Q.	1 pc., 3/4" × 1 1/4" × 18 1/2"
B.	3 pcs., 3/4" × 10" × 43 1/2"		R.	1 pc., 3/4" × 17" × 28 1/4"
C.	1 pc., 3/4" × 9 1/2" × 43 1/2"		S.	2 pcs., 1/2" × 1/2" × 19"
D.	1 pc., 1/2" × 20 1/2" × 45"		T.	2 pcs., 1/2" × 1/2" × 15"
E.	2 pcs., 1 1/2" × 1 1/2" × 43 1/2"		U.	1 pc., 3/4" × 8" × 26"
F.	1 pc., 3/4" × 31 1/4" × 43 1/2"		V.	1 pc., 3/4" × 11" × 26"
G.	4 pcs., 3/4" × 1 1/2" × 43 1/2"		W.	2 pcs., 1/4" × 16" × 20"
H.	2 pcs., 3/4" × 32" × 45"		X.	1 pc., 3/4" × 10 1/4" × 19 1/4"
I.	1 pc., 3/4" × 18 1/2" × 14"		Y.	1 pc., 3/4" × 10 1/4" × 14"
J.	2 pcs., 3/4" × 18 1/2" × 32"		Z.	2 pcs., 3/4" × 1 1/2" × 19"
K.	1 pc., 3/4" × 18 1/2" × 29 1/4"		AA.	1 pc., 3/8" × 6" × 24 5/8"
L.	1 pc., 3/4" × 18 1/2" × 13 1/2"		BB.	1 pc., 1/4" × 25" × 18"
M.	2 pcs., 1 1/2" × 1 1/2" × 29 1/4"		CC.	4 pcs., 1/4" × 1" × 18"
N.	2 pcs., 1 1/2" × 1 1/2" × 15 1/2"		DD.	2 pcs., 3/8" × 6" × 18"
			EE.	1 pc., 3/4" × 2" × 6"
O.	2 pcs., 3/4" × 1 1/2" × 18 1/2"		FF.	1 pc., 3/4" × 6 7/8" × 18"
P.	1 pc., 3/4" × 2 1/2" × 18 1/2"		GG.	2 pcs., 3/16" × 14 1/4" × 24"

installed; drawer guides (P,Q) are nailed to the side panels (I,J); and top panels (K) and (L) lie flush with the tops of seat and bin frames, (H,I) and (H,J) respectively. Note also that one drawer guide (P) is twice as wide as other guide (Q) to clear the width of the frame (H). The drawer is standard drawer construction, and the storage bin's front panel (V) is hinged to the bottom of the framework (H) to tilt out easily. The drawer has double runners (CC) on each side. The storage bin section—perfect for use as a laundry hamper—is completed with decorative trim (S,T) nailed around the top.

Chapter 4

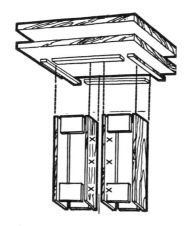

Backyard Projects

This chapter contains projects for the backyard to suit every member of your family. You'll find a sun deck, decorative benches, an equipment shed, and even a space-age playhouse for the children. All are guaranteed to make outdoor living an exciting experience for the whole family!

ACCENT YOUR BACKYARD WITH DECORATIVE BENCHES

These contoured benches that double as storage lockers will accent any level pool or patio section of your backyard (Fig. 4-1). They are designed to form a practical and pleasant border, which makes them ideal for setting off different parts of the yard. You could build them to divide a children's play area from your lawn or pool, for example.

An easy construction plan for this project would be to first prefabricate all of the side and top or lid sections, then join these sections into the three separate bench units, and finally join the separate units into the completed contoured bench. See Fig. 4-2 and Table 4-1.

In prefabricating the four long front and rear sections, for example, you would nail outside frame pieces (C,C,C) or (D,D,D) to four vertical support cleats (H), starting at one end and spacing the cleats on 2-foot centers. Note that one end of the longer sections made with boards (C) will be without an (H) support, since the longer sides will be supported where they overlap the front and back of the center bench section in the completed bench.

The center bench unit sections are prefabricated in the same way by nailing outside surface pieces (B,B,B,B) or (E,E,E) to inside support cleats (G,G) or (I,I,I). The extra supporting cleat (J) which is shown in Fig. 4-2 is nailed to the underside of the center top pieces (B,B,B,B) to give this section more support.

When you join the prefabricated sections into the separate bench units, toenail the ground and upper end supports (I) to the corresponding side cleats (either H in the case of the long units or G where the center unit is being assembled). Now, before you attach the lid (A,A,A,A) and top center sections

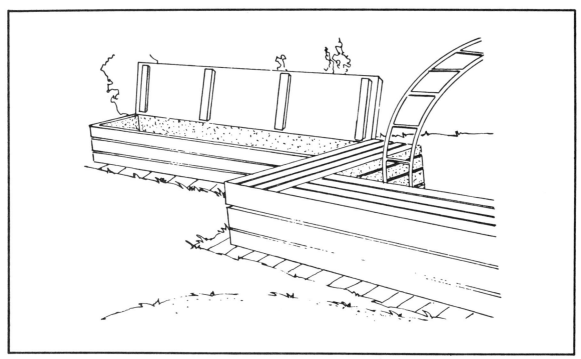

Fig. 4-1. Decorative benches for the backyard.

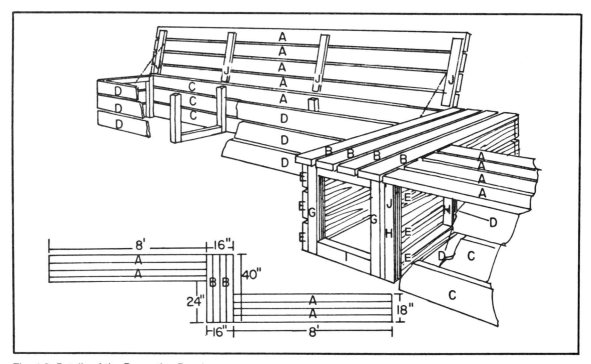

Fig. 4-2. Details of the Decorative Benches.

Table 4-1. Materials for the Decorative Benches.

A.	8 pcs, 3/4″ × 3 1/2″ × 96″	F.	6 pcs, 3/4″ × 5 1/2″ × 14 1/2″
B.	4 pcs, 3/4″ × 3 1/2″ × 40″	G.	8 pcs, 1 1/2″ × 1 1/2″ × 18″
C.	6 pcs, 3/4″ × 3 1/2″ × 112″	H.	12 pcs, 1 1/2″ × 1 1/2″ × 17 1/4″
D.	6 pcs, 3/4″ × 5 1/2″ × 96″	I.	14 pcs, 1 1/2″ × 1 1/2″ × 11
E.	6 pcs, 3/4″ × 5 1/2″ × 38 1/2″	J.	9 pcs, 3/4″ × 1 1/2″ × 14″ 1/2″

(B,B,B,B), nail the assembled side units to the center unit to form the complete bench shell.

Use either finishing nails or small-headed screw nails when you do the prefabricating, but try heavier common nails when you toe the sections together and join the bench units into one. You can either counterset the exposed nail heads and putty them, or prime and paint over them without countersetting. A few coats of a good wood preservative and stain in redwood or some other color will give the benches a lasting and outdoor-looking finish.

Use three large butt hinges for each lid, countersinking the bottom leaf. The metal handle or pull seen at the front of the right-hand lid is available in any hardware store.

A level bed, such as you could put together with bricks and sand, or at least a base of tamped earth, will give strength to the bench unit and make it more permanent. The brick and sand bed would provide excellent drainage as well.

USE EXTRA GARAGE STORAGE SPACE

Here's a nice easy project that requires no great skill in carpentry and provides twin movable cabinets with storage space for game equipment or for automotive tools and accessories (Fig. 4-3). An interesting feature of these cabinets is that they make use of the space between cars in a double garage, which is almost never used. Equipped with casters, the cabinets can be moved out of the way if you need to work on the cars from the inner side.

Refer to Fig. 4-4 and Table 4-2. All parts are fastened together with butt joints using glue and nails. Except for the vertical partitions in the center, the nails should be 1 1/2-inch counterset

finishing nails, and the holes filled with wood putty.

The horizontals (A,D,D,A) are each a single piece. Those in the middle (D,D) are fastened to the sides with nails driven through G and H. The top and bottom pieces (A,A) are held in place with nails driven through them into the ends of G and H.

All the horizontals are notched at one end to fit around the square column in the middle of the garage. The column in your garage may be round, in which case make your notch to fit this shape. The notches can easily be made with a coping or saber saw. The bottom of each cabinet rests on a frame made up of 1 × 4s. The shorter pieces (C) are attached to the under sides of the long pieces (B).

The upper partition (J) is fastened with nails driven through the top of A and the bottom of D. The same method should be used for the bottom partition (E). The middle partition (F), however, requires a somewhat different method of fastening. First, be sure that it fits tightly between the two middle shelves (D,D). Apply glue to the upper and lower edges and tap it into place with a mallet or hammer and wood block. Use a few 3/4-inch brads to toenail the upper and lower edges.

The perforated hardboard back is fastened to the back edges of the shelves, partitions, and outside frame with glue and 1 1/4-inch finishing nails.

A pair of hooks and eyes can be used in the narrow space between the two cabinets to prevent them from rolling away from the post. Finish should be a good grade of enamel applied over a wood primer or shellac diluted 50 percent with alcohol.

ADD A BACKYARD GARDEN SUN DECK

Summertime living means outdoor living. With a pleasant sun deck that blends in with your backyard

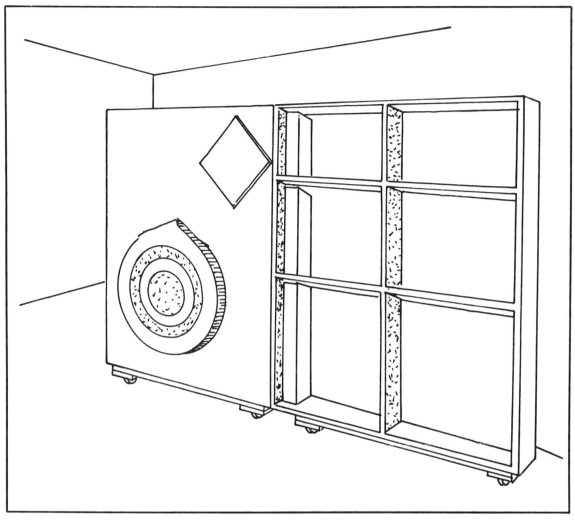

Fig. 4-3. Storage space for game equipment or tools and accessories.

planting nicely, such as the one shown in Fig. 4-5, you can get a panoramic view of your garden while enjoying the summer sun.

This deck or garden platform is set on slightly sloping ground with the rear almost at ground level and the front up a few steps. The platform is made up of four squares, but could vary depending on your particular needs.

Refer to Fig. 4-6 and Table 4-3. Redwood is the main type of wood used. The rough timbers which come in contact with the earth, such as F,G,H,I,J, should be soaked in creosote or penta to resist

decay and termite damage. These pieces could be Douglas fir or whatever wood your lumber dealer supplies in large timbers. This platform, however, is supported on pieces of used railroad ties. As shown in Fig. 4-5, the first steps, which simply lie on the ground, are also railroad ties. These first steps are optional and are therefore not shown in Fig. 4-6. You may prefer to have only two steps, or you can make a third step like the other two.

When you are building the platform, make sure that the foundation pieces (G,J) are perfectly level. Once these pieces are set in 8- × -16-inch "puddles"

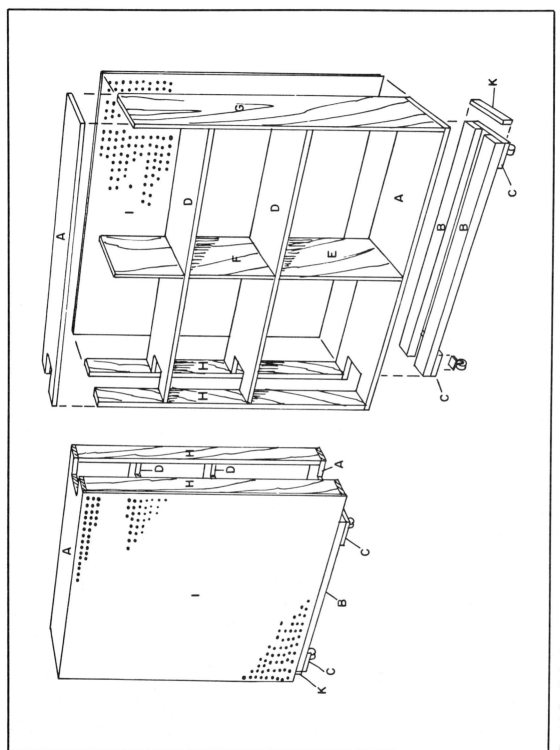

Fig. 4-4. Details for the garage storage unit.

Table 4-2. Materials for the Garage Storage Space.

A. 4 pcs, 3/4″ × 9 1/4″ × 47 1/2″
B. 4 pcs, 1 1/2″ × 2 1/2″ × 40″
C. 4 pcs, 3/4″ × 3 1/2″ × 8 1/2″
D. 4 pcs, 3/4″ × 9 1/4″ × 46″
E. 2 pcs, 3/4″ × 9 1/4″ × 23 1/2″
F. 2 pcs, 3/4″ × 9 1/4″ × 17″
G. 2 pcs, 3/4″ × 9 1/4″ × 56″
H. 4 pcs, 3/4″ × 1 5/8″ × 56″
I. 2 pcs, 47 1/2″ × 57 1/2″
pegboard
J. 2 pcs, 3/4″ × 9 1/4″ × 14″
K. 2 pcs, 3/4″ × 1 1/2″ × 8 1/2″

WHAT TO BUY

16′ of 3/4″ × 10″ boards
14′ of 2″ × 3″'s
6′ of 1″ × 4″
1 pegboard, 4′ × 8′
1 pegboard, 4′ × 4′

Fig. 4-5. Backyard Garden Sun Deck.

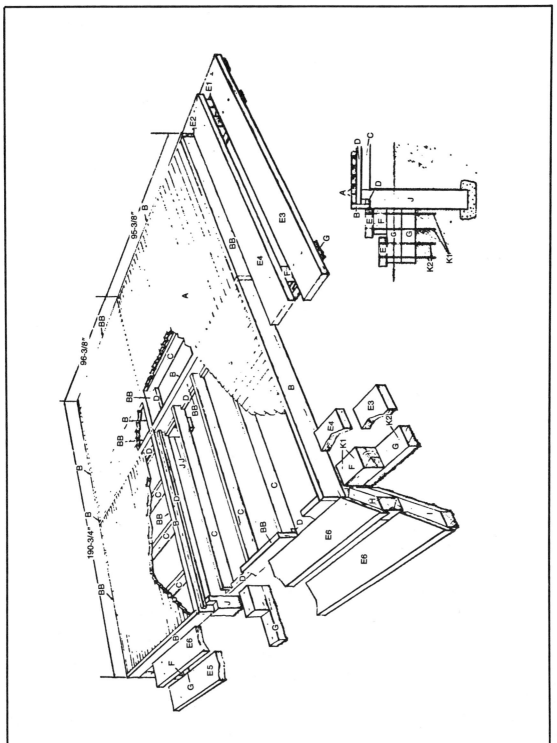

Fig. 4-6. Details of the Backyard Garden Sun Deck.

77

Table 4-3. Materials for the Backyard Garden Sun Deck.

A.	100 pcs, each: 92 3/8″ × 3 1/2″ × 1 1/2″		G.	12 pcs, each: 22 1/2″ × 7 1/4″ × 5 1/2″
B.	8 pcs, each: 95 3/8″ × 7 1/4″ × 1 1/2″		H.	2 pcs, each: 14″ × 7 1/4″ × 5 1/2″
C.	12 pcs, each: 92 3/8″ × 5 1/2″ × 1 1/2″		I.	4 pcs, each: 30″ × 7 1/4″ × 5 1/2″
D.	16 pcs, each: 92 3/8″ × 1 1/2″ × 1 1/2″		J.	8 pcs, each: 46″ × 7 1/4″ × 5 1/2″
E1.	1 pc, 96″ × 11 1/4″ × 2 1/2″		K1.	20 zinc-coated threaded steel rods, each: 27″ × 1/2″ (diameter)
E2.	1 pc, 84 3/4″ × 11 1/4″ × 2 1/2″		K2.	20 zinc-coated threaded steel rods, each: 21″ × 1/2″ (diameter)
E3.	1 pc, 235 3/4″ × 11 1/4″ × 2 1/2″		BB.	8 pcs, each: 92 3/8″ × 7 1/4″ × 1 1/2″
E4.	1 pc, 213 1/2″ × 11 1/4″ × 2 1/2″		JJ.	1 pc, 41 3/4″ × 7 1/4″ × 5 1/2″
E5.	1 pc, 211 3/4″ × 11 1/4″ × 2 1/2″			
E6.	1 pc, 200 1/2″ × 11 1/4″ × 2 1/2″			
F.	6 pcs, each: 10 1/2″ × 7 1/4″ × 5 1/2″			

of concrete, the entire platform is level. Following placement of the foundation posts, it's a good idea to proceed to the other outer pieces, such as H,I, and the E items.

When you get to the point of nailing deck boards (A), you can get automatic spacing for them by inserting a 3/16-inch piece of plywood between them before driving home the nails. The frame (B,BB) is toenailed to piece J using cement-coated nails. Note that the foundation post (JJ) is 4 1/4 inches shorter than the other eight posts and is not notched so as to provide room on it for all four frame corners. The four sections making up the deck or platform are bolted together with zinc-plated 1/2- × -3 1/2-inch bolts, nuts, and washers.

Step stringers (F,G) are held together with zinc-plated 1/2-inch threaded steel rods (K1, K2). Corner pieces (H,I) are secured to the garden steps with zinc-plated 1/2- × -3 1/2-inch lag bolts and washers, counter-bored and plugged.

Paint nuts, bolts, and washers with two coats of exterior-grade flat black paint. All the redwood is clear, heart grades, used with bark sides up and bleached with two coats of bleaching oil to prevent it from turning black as it weathers. The deck is surrounded by a mulch of broken bark. You may, however, prefer to have grass of other plantings in this area. For a sense of texture and contrast, you can also use crushed bluestone or gravel.

BUILD AN EQUIPMENT SHED

A shed in which you can store all your garden tools and outdoor equipment is a great convenience for any homeowner, so when Jerry Stasse of New Jersey got himself a small riding mower, he decided to build a shed for it in his backyard. What Stasse put up is a very soundly built frame structure that measures 10 × 16 feet (Fig. 4-7). It is a rather attractive barn red structure with white trim, and looks almost too nice to be just a shed.

The floor, siding, and roof deck are made of a strong, dense, wood fiber board that resists moisture, fungus, rot, and termites. Made by the Homasote Co. from recycled waste newspaper, this material is light and splinter-free and has excellent insulating properties.

Stasse began by nailing 2- × -6 floor joists together. The joists (beams) rest on piles rather than on a concrete foundation. The Homasote floor decking comes in pieces which are 2 feet wide, 8 feet long, and 1 3/8 inches (actual 1 11/32 inches) thick and has tongues or grooves all around (Fig. 4-8). It was nailed directly to the joists with annular

Fig. 4-7. Equipment Shed.

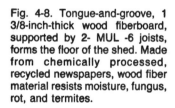Fig. 4-8. Tongue-and-groove, 1
3/8-inch-thick wood fiberboard,
supported by 2- MUL -6 joists,
forms the floor of the shed. Made
from chemically processed,
recycled newspapers, wood fiber
material resists moisture, fungus,
rot, and termites.

thread nails that have barbs on the shank to make them hold more tightly than ordinary nails (Fig. 4-9). All edges where tongues and grooves meet are supported by framing.

With the floor completed, the next step was the walls. They were made up of the usual 2 × 4s spaced 16 inches on centers (16 inches from the middle of one 2 × 4 to the middle of the next 2 × 4) (Fig. 4-10). Double 2 × 6s were used as headers or lintels above the door and the single window. The door and window jambs (sides) consist of double 2 × 4s, as is required in most frame construction. The horizontal beams (top plates) that join all the vertical studs of the walls are also doubled. Since this is a relatively light structure, the rafters (roof beams) are 2 × 4s instead of the usual 2 × 6s or 2 × 8s.

The siding is made of the same material as the floor but comes in 1-×-8 sheets 11/32 inch thick and is primed with white paint on one side (Fig. 4-11). These sheets were nailed to the framing, paint side out, with 1 1/2-inch, annular-thread, corrosion-resistant nails. Proper spacing of nails is very important, not only to get the best results, but also to pass inspection by the local building inspector. Following the manufacturer's instructions, Stasse spaced his nails 6 to 8 inches along the edges and 12 to 14 inches inside each sheet (Fig. 4-12).

Next, Stasse nailed the roof decking to the rafters. The deck material consisted of panels similar to the flooring, 1 3/8 inches thick and 2 feet × 8 feet with tongues and grooves on opposite sides (Fig. 4-13). Here again, proper nailing is important. Following the manufacturer's instructions, Stasse used five nails per rafter, about 4 1/2 inches apart and 3/4 inch back from the edges.

The roof deck was covered with asphalt strip shingles with every other row staggered to offset the cutouts of the shingles below (Fig. 4-14). A double-hung wood window was then nailed into place in the window opening. Exterior moldings were nailed around the window and the nail heads countersunk and puttied.

All cracks and joints in the siding, including those around the window moldings, were carefully caulked with a cartridge caulking gun (Fig. 4-15). The siding was painted red with a good grade of water-based exterior paint (Fig. 4-16). The window

Fig. 4-9. Nail wood fiberboard to joists underneath. The nails, which have barbs on the shank to make them hold better, are driven at 6-inch intervals.

Fig. 4-10. Completed framing for the walls and roof. The 2-×-4 framing is spaced 16 inches on center. The rafters are also 2 × 4s.

Fig. 4-11. Wood fiber, 4-×-8 sheets, 15/32 inches thick and primed with white paint on one side, are now ready to be fastened to the framing.

Fig. 4-12. Nailing of sheets to the framing is completed. Nails are spaced 6 to 8 inches along the edges and 12 to 14 inches on the inside.

Fig. 4-13. Tongue-and-groove 2-×-8 sheets, 1 3/8 inches thick, are nailed to the rafters to form the roof deck.

Fig. 4-14. The roof shingling is completed. White asphalt strip shingles, in staggered rows, were nailed directly to the roof deck.

Fig. 4-15. Sealing of all cracks in the siding material where the sheets meet is done with a caulking gun, which contains a cartridge of caulk.

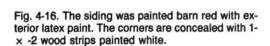

Fig. 4-16. The siding was painted barn red with exterior latex paint. The corners are concealed with 1-× -2 wood strips painted white.

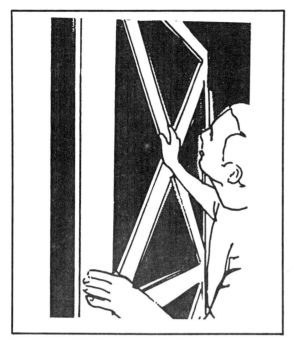

Fig. 4-17. A lightweight door is made from siding material, with 1 × 4s nailed around the edges on both sides and as cross bracing in front.

and all trim were painted white. Corner joints were concealed by 1-×-2-inch wood strips previously painted white.

The attractively decorative sliding door put together by Stasse deserves special mention. Made of the 11/32-inch siding material with 1 × 4s nailed to its front and back surfaces, this door is light, strong, and rigid, as well as good looking (Fig. 4-17). It hangs from a pair of rollers on an overhead track and rolls to the left when opened. A wood strip nailed to the siding acts as a stop to prevent the door from rolling too far to the left and falling off the track.

Finally, wood strips, or battens, were painted white and then nailed to the siding to conceal vertical cracks and to complete the decorative scheme (see Fig. 4-18).

PRODUCE A PORTABLE WORKBENCH

Many plans exist for the construction of workbenches. Often, however, they don't suit the novice hobbyist, who can't imagine wrestling with com-

plicated instructions. Neither do they suit the experienced handyman seeking an easy-to-build spacious place to work, or the handyman living in an apartment.

The workbench here is a good solution. It can be built in 3 hours from two sheets of plywood and three strips of pine, using only a hammer, hand drill with a 1/2-inch bit, and a bottle of glue (Fig. 4-19).

You will get a 5-foot by 30-inch workspace on a bench sturdy enough for medium-duty work, such as holding a portable drill press. If you live in an apartment and move fairly often, you'll never lose any bench parts. There are only three components—a benchtop and two supports—for easy portability and reassembly (Fig. 4-20).

The hardest part of the whole project is cutting the plywood and pine.

The Cutting

At the lumberyard, buy two sheets of 3/4-inch interior grade plywood in the standard 4-×-8-foot size. Interior grade has one side finished, the other

Fig. 4-18. Battens, painted white, are nailed to the siding, both for decorative effect and to conceal vertical cracks.

Fig. 4-19. You can make this sturdy workbench in 3 hours or less from two sheets of plywood and three strips of pine, using only a hammer, hand drill with a 1/-inch bit, and bottle of glue.

Fig. 4-20. The bench has three furniture-sized sections for easy portability, a plus for apartment residents who relocate often and the handyman who needs to work in various areas.

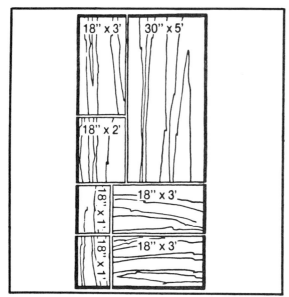

Fig. 4-21. Cutting diagram for 4-×-8-foot plywood. Cut two sheets the same way.

You'll also need: 1/4 lb. each of 2-inch and 1 1/4-inch nails with heads; three 1/2-inch diameter, 2-inch long stove bolts with nuts and flat washers, and two sheets of medium grit sandpaper.

Then, as Figs. 4-21 through 4-23 show, cut lumber as follows:

- Along the width, cut two pieces. Make each piece 18 inches wide by 4 feet long.
- Along the length, cut one piece, 18 inches wide by 5 feet long.
- Cut 1 foot from each 4-foot piece.
- Cut 2 feet from the 5-foot piece.

When both sheets are cut exactly the same way, you have the following: two pieces 30 inches wide by 5 feet long, six pieces, 18 inches wide × 3 feet long; two pieces 18 inches wide by 2 feet long; and four pieces, 18 inches wide by 1 foot long. Make further cuts in two of the 18-inch-×-1-foot pieces. First cut 1 1/2 inches from the ends, making each piece 16 1/2 inches × 1 foot. Then cut each piece in half along the length to give

unfinished. Also buy enough 1-×-2-inch pine to cut two pieces 3 feet long, and two pieces 22 inches long.

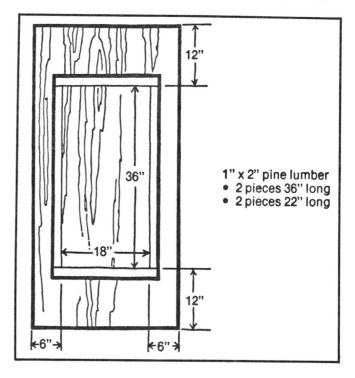

Fig. 4-22. Bench top diagram (underside view).

1" x 2" pine lumber
- 2 pieces 36" long
- 2 pieces 22" long

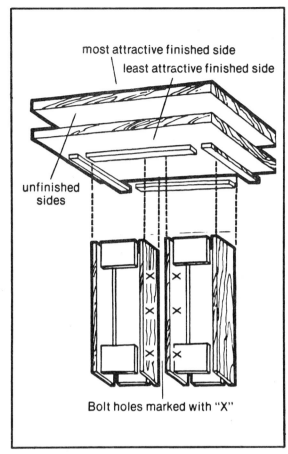

Fig. 4-23. Exploded diagram of the workbench.

you four pieces, each one measuring 16 1/2 × 6 inches.

The 18-inch by 1-foot pieces you did not cut will help make the bench. The 18-inch by 2-foot pieces are scrap.

The Supports

Your time spent buying lumber and other materials possibly totalled 1 hour, and it shouldn't take more than 1 hour to build the supports. The benchtop can also be made in 1 hour or less.

Your first job is to construct the bench supports. To help you, nail the two 18-inch by 1-foot pieces into an L-shaped "minibench" 18 inches high.

Place one 18-inch- × -3-foot piece on the minibench as shown in Fig. 4-24, then spread glue along the edge of another piece. Place the glued edge under the piece on the minibench and nail the pieces together with 2-inch nails.

Figure 4-25 illustrates how the edges should be placed when gluing and nailing. After two pieces are together, push the minibench far enough under the top piece so you can attach the other side of this support.

Now for the front. Using glue and 2-inch nails, attach one 16 1/2- × -6-inch piece at the top of the support and another at the bottom (see Fig. 4-25 for placement). Follow these same directions when making the second support.

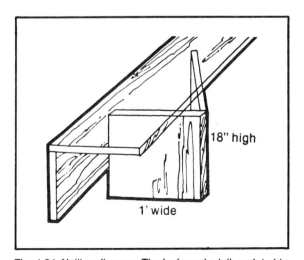

Fig. 4-24. Nailing diagram. The L-shaped minibench holds support pieces when you are gluing and nailing.

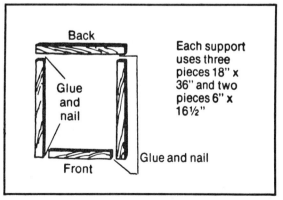

Fig. 4-25. The bench support gluing diagram (top view). Both supports are glued the same way.

The Benchtop

To make the benchtop, first examine the finished sides of the two 30-inch-×-5-foot plywood pieces. One will probably look more attractive than the order—this is the side you want to face up when the bench is complete.

For construction, this side should be facing down, as the piece lies on the floor. Spread glue liberally on the unfinished side. Then place the second 30-inch-×-5-foot piece, unfinished side down, on the glue. The two pieces must be in line with each other on all sides. Glue will make large pieces adhere fairly well even when the glue is wet, so you might need help with this step.

Then stand up. You're now looking at the underside of your benchtop. Hammer in your 1 1/4-inch nails all around, 3 inches from the edge and about 8 inches apart. Do not kneel on the wood while nailing; you'll make the pieces slide on the glue. Finally, hammer in 1 1/4-inch nails along the length down the center.

Your next step involves the 1-×-2-inch pine strips. When the bench is assembled, the benchtop's weight will prevent it from rocking on the supports, and the pine strips will keep it from slipping off.

To get the strips on correctly, first examine the two edges along the benchtop's 5-foot length. The more attractive edge should be facing you when the bench is assembled. Place the supports side by side, fronts facing in that direction, on the benchtop underside.

When in place, the supports must together measure 12 inches from each end and 6 inches from front and back (Fig. 4-26). Scribe a pencil line all around them, then remove them to one side off the benchtop. Spread glue along the pine strips and place them outside the pencil line, as shown in Fig. 4-22. Hammer them down with 1 1/4-inch nails.

The Assembly

A few more steps and construction is complete. The

Fig. 4-26. The bench top sits on supports without being bolted down; so centering is important for stability. The overhang must measure 12 inches at each end and 6 inches at front and back.

Fig. 4-27. The workbench setup is a 5-minute job. Place supports side by side. Bolt them together. Then slide the top over, using pine strips as a guide. Vise and outlets are optional.

supports will be bolted together, so mark a centerline down one side of each support (Fig. 4-27). Mark points at 6, 18, and 30 inches on each line, then drill 1/2-inch holes at each point. The bolts you bought will fit through the holes.

Smooth all bench surfaces, edges, and corners with sandpaper. Bolt the supports together and slide the benchtop over them until if falls into place. Your workbench is done!

There are optional steps which can extend your project over 2 days: coating the supports and benchtop with clear varnish, adding a vise and power tool extension outlets, and building drawers or shelves which will fit into the supports. Even though it is quickly and easily constructed, this bench is sturdy work furniture.

BUILD A SPACE-AGE PLAYHOUSE

Have the kids been nagging you about that playhouse you promised them? Here's one that's not only easy to build but will be the envy of every child in the neighborhood, including those who already have playhouses (Fig. 4-28). The design of the house is simple. It takes only a few days to build, requires almost no upkeep, can take most of the abuse most ordinary kids would give it, and is cheaper than most ready-made playhouses.

Since the design of the house is so simple (Fig. 4-29), it'll not only easily fit in with most surroundings, but a careful examination of it will show how closely it resembles that spindly-legged gadget that took the astronauts to the moon. Add a coat-hanger antenna and pie-plate radar dish, and your children's imagination will take off on a flight of fancy to the moon.

No playhouse, no matter how well constructed, is going to last forever—but at least this one will go a long way toward fulfilling your children's need for a playhouse for several years. One word of caution, however: this playhouse is not too well-suited to areas that have heavy winters, although it can withstand most weathering.

You'll need a level area of about 8 square feet, preferably in the back of your house, to build the

Fig. 4-28. The Space-Age Playhouse.

playhouse. Its overall dimensions are approximately 10 feet high by about 4 feet wide by about 6 feet long (Table 4-4). Though most of the house can be built of pine, for the structural members that come in contact with the earth, use lumber that has been pressure-treated to resist decay and termite damage. Some of the western woods, such as Douglas fir, western red cedar, ponderosa pine, or similar woods, are best.

The house lends itself easily to climbing by children. Rather than let it remain mobile, in which case it could possibly tip over, fix the six long legs (A) in concrete. No elaborate foundation is required—six holes about 15 inches deep are sufficient. The vertical 2 × 2s (A,I,P) are on 24-inch centers. After wedging the 2-× -2 stock in the earth, fix them in place with enough concrete to furnish about a 6-inch anchor on all sides of each piece. Allow at least two days for the concrete to cure before proceeding with the final construction.

The frame should be completed before you add any other structural members. Use countersunk

Table 4-4. Materials for the Space-Age Playhouse.

A.	6 pcs, each: 120″ × 2″ × 2″
B.	4 pcs, each: 74″ × 4″ × 1″
C.	2 pcs, each: 60″ × 2″ × 1″
D.	4 pcs, each: 50″ × 2″ × 1″
E.	1 pc, 46″ × 4″ × 1″
F.	2 pcs, each: 50″ × 4″ × 1″
G.	2 pcs, each: 22 1/2″ × 4″ × 1″
H.	1 pc, 42″ × 2″ × 2″
I.	5 pcs, each: 69″ × 2″ × 2″
J.	12 pcs, each: 22″ × 2″ × 2″ (1 not shown)
K.	3 pcs, each: 22 1/4″ × 4″ × 2″ (2 not shown)
L.	3 pcs, each: 53″ × 23 3/4″ × 1/8″ (1 not shown)
M.	4 pcs, each: 57″ × 23″ × 1/8″
N.	2 pcs, each: 46″ × 46″ × 3/4″
O.	3 pcs, each: 26″ × 2″ × 1″
P.	1 pc, 57″ × 2″ × 2″
Q.	2 pcs, each: 74″ × 2″ × 1″
R.	2 pcs, each: 52″ × 2″ × 1″
S.	25 pcs, each: 22 1/4″ × 2″ × 1″ (some not shown)

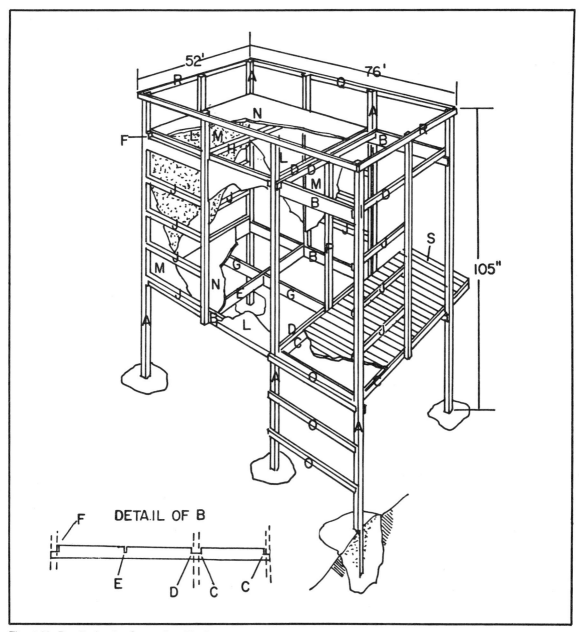

Fig. 4-29. Details for the Space-Age Playhouse.

screws with wood filler to complete it. You could also use nails. All pieces except those joined to B are secured with either butt or flat joints. Pieces joined to B are secured with lap joints. You should build the two long pieces (B) first, tying them together with four cross members (C,D,F). Cross-brace these pieces temporarily to keep the frame square and set it in its permanent footings. The four sides of the playhouse enclosure are built to the same specification, that is, on 24-inch centers. About the most complicated cuts you'll have to make are in piece B, into which are fitted several

91

pieces (E,F,G), as shown in the Fig. 4-29. Bear in mind that these cuts must allow space, not only for securing them to the upright pieces, but also for cross members such as D and C.

After you have put the frame together, but before you add the walls, roof, and flooring, be sure to seal thoroughly all wood surfaces with regular house paint that matches the color scheme of your home and yard. The walls, flooring, and roof consist of sheets of hardboard or any other material that withstands weathering, such as vinyl plastic sheets. The hardboard is inserted in 1/2-inch slots in the vertical 2 × 2s and nailed or screwed from the inside. Roof and floor (N) are 3/4-inch plywood nailed or screwed all around to B,C,D,E,F, and G. A single 2 × 2 (H) is used under the roof to increase headroom instead of crossed 1 × 4s (E,G) such as are used under the floor. The reason is fairly obvious: it will bear more weight.

Although it is not indicated in the drawing, it might also be a good idea to use the same construction for the roof as for the floor if you expect your kids to go climbing all over the roof, too. In this case, use some good, stout, 3/4-inch plywood.

Chapter 5

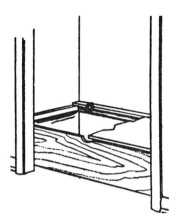

Storage Projects

Need an extra closet? Don't have the space you need to store the things you have? This chapter will open your eyes to exciting possibilities for storage from space you already have. You can use an empty wall, the bottom of closets, and many more places you never knew you could for storage for every room in your house.

CONSTRUCT CREATIVE CLOSETRY

A small room that's unusually deep can yield a surprising amount of storage that's entirely out of the way. The secret is to set up shelving across the back end of the room, from the floor all the way to the ceiling, then to seal it off at the front with an attractive permanent wall and handsome louver bifold doors (Fig. 5-1).

Shelving was planned to separate the contents by purpose. The room depth of 12 feet allowed plenty of depth, but a 3-foot space for the shelves was deemed adequate.

To save work, panels of 3/4-inch fir plywood were cut to the 3-foot width, and installed over fir

cleats spiked to the wall studs on either side (Figs. 5-2 and 5-3). In effect, there are four shelves. The bottom shelf is really a platform laid over 2- x -4 furring over the cement slab and linoleum floor.

The second shelf is 31 inches higher (measured to the bottom face); the third is 20 inches above the second; and the top shelf is up another 16 inches. The latter is recessed halfway back, for easy access.

Despite their heft, plywood panels are far from rigid for so wide a span. In fact, they bowed considerably, even when loaded lightly. Vertical braces set between shelves, however, kept the latter in line.

The next step was to conceal all those shelves and their polyglot contents. Bifold louver doors made of western hemlock were chosen for their crisp good looks and to allow air circulation. The bifold units, each 29 1/2 inches in width, open to only half of that into the small room. Stock hemlock and fir bifold louvered doors are widely available from lumberyards.

One awkward obstacle interfered with the new

Fig. 5-1. Closet for a small, deep room.

Fig. 5-2. Nail 1- x -2 cleats to side walls through the plaster-board and into the studs behind the plasterboard.

Fig. 5-3. Plywood sheets are trimmed to shelf size and laid on the cleats. Brads are used to fasten the shelves to the cleats.

94

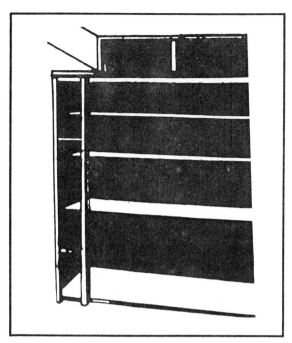

Fig. 5-4. An opening for bifold doors is roughed out and framed with 2 × 4s, skirting the heating duct in the upper left.

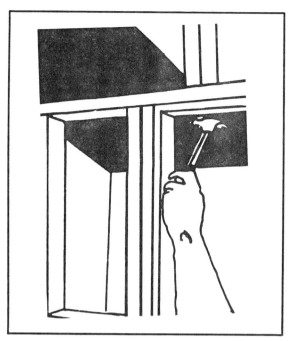

Fig. 5-5. The jamb and the header, which line the rough doorway framing of the 2 × 4s, are nailed into place.

wall, which was needed to support the doors and conceal the 20 inches or more of width that the doors couldn't cover, and that was a boxed-in heat duct in the upper left corner, 19 inches across and 12 inches from bottom to top.

The key to the framing were two horizontal 2 × 4s, one against the ceiling and nailed to joists above, and the second below the heat duct and extending from wall to wall (Fig. 5-4). The latter's height is measured for the bifold doors, plus the thickness of door jamb and the overhead door track (Fig. 5-5).

Vertical framing included pieces against the walls, then two for the sides of the door opening, spaced for the side jambs and clearance for the bifolds.

The door opening was placed to the right side, instead of at dead center, because of the heat duct offset. Bottom pivot brackets were made to screw into the framing and didn't require fastening into the cement floor (Fig. 5-6).

For the wall facing, 1- × -4-inch tongue-and-groove flush-joint hemlock boards were selected to

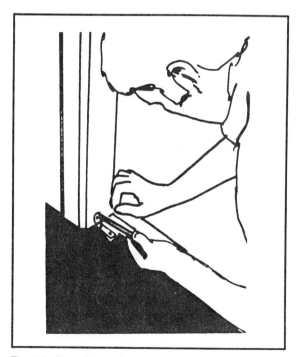

Fig. 5-6. Pivot fixtures for the bifold louvered doors are installed at the bottoms of the jambs on both sides.

Fig. 5-7. Tongue-and-groove hemlock boards are nailed over the framing to form a wall to the left of the door opening.

make a handsome handcrafted surround for the bifold doors (Figs. 5-7 and 5-8). They're as easy to trim and install in small sections at the sides and across the top as any other material.

Two kinds of moldings finished the carpentry: 2 1/4-inch casing set 1/4 inch out from the forward edge of the side and top jambs, and 1-×-1-inch pieces to conceal the overhead track (Figs. 5-9 and 5-10).

ADD A SHELF UNIT FOR AN ALCOVE

Got a nice alcove around one of your windows? Here's how to make an attractive shelf unit that will fit inside it. Add an attractive window shade like the one in Fig. 5-11, and you've got a striking unit with ample storage space. Of course, you don't actually have to have an alcove to make this good looking shelf and cabinet arrangement.

Refer to Table 5-1 and Fig. 5-12. The shelves are all joined with simple butt joints. White glue and 1 1/2-inch finishing nails are used for all joints. The nails are driven through the sides of the ver-

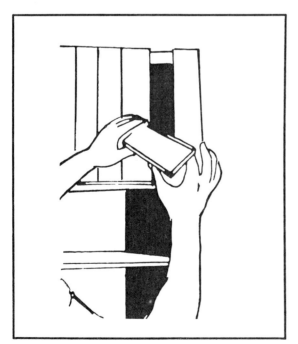

Fig. 5-8. The space between the ceiling and the top of the closet is walled off with tongue-and-groove hemlock boards.

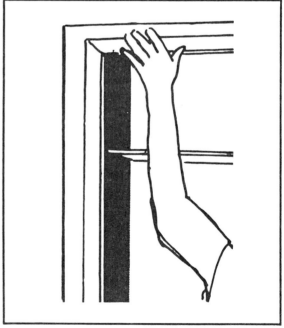

Fig. 5-9. The side and top moldings are nailed in place 1/4 inch back from the opening. Note the flat molding strips on the shelf edges.

Fig. 5-10. The upper track is installed and doors are hung on pivots in the track. Strips measuring 1 × 1 hide the track and finish the job.

Fig. 5-11. Shelf unit for an alcove.

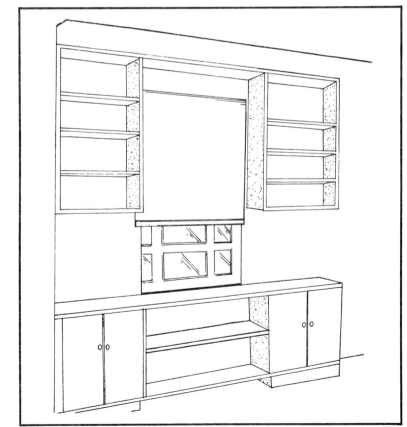

Table 5-1. Materials for the Shelf Unit for an Alcove.

A. 1 pc, 3/4″ × 7 1/2″ × 92″
B. 4 pcs, 3/4″ × 7 1/2″ × 40″
C. 2 pcs, 3/4″ × 9 1/2″ × 92″
D. 10 pcs, angle irons
E. 4 pcs, 3/4″ × 4″ × 26 1/2″

F. 8 pcs, 3/4″ × 7 1/2″ × 26 1/2″
G. 4 pcs, 3/4″ × 13 1/4″ × 22 1/2″
H. 1 pc, 3/4″ × 9 1/2″ × 36″
I. 4 pcs, 3/4″ × 4″ × 7 3/4″
J. 4 pcs, 3/4″ × 9 1/2″ × 22 1/2″

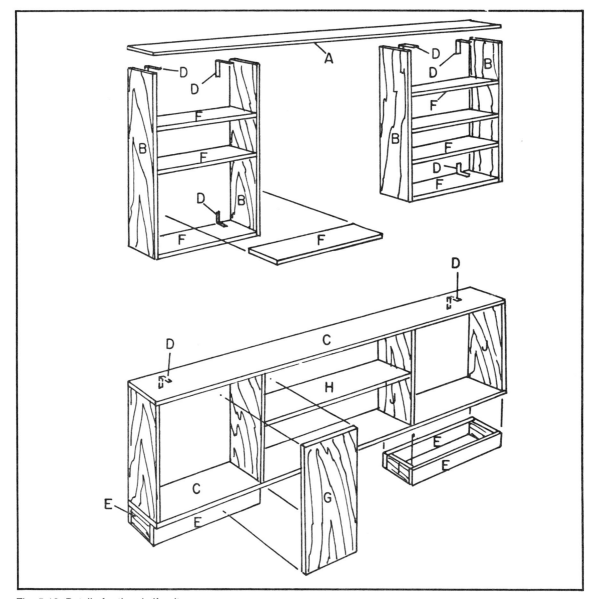

Fig. 5-12. Details for the shelf unit.

ticals (B) into the ends of the shelves and counter-sunk. Putty is then used to fill the nail holes. The upper shelves are put together as single units and are then joined together by a single board (A) nailed and glued to the four verticals (B).

The way you fasten the upper shelves to the wall depends on what the walls are made of. If they are masonry walls, drill holes with a carbide-tipped bit and insert fiber plugs for 4-inch angle braces. These braces should be located in the upper right- and left-hand corners of both shelf assemblies directly under the top board (A).

Another two pairs of angle braces should be placed in the lower left- and lower right-hand corners. If the walls have wood studs, the screws holding the braces should be driven into these.

The shelf and cabinet assembly on the floor has two long boards (C,C) which span the width of the alcove and form the top and bottom of both cabinets. The sides of the cabinets (J) are nailed through the top and bottom of these two boards. The center shelf (H) is held in place with glue and finishing nails driven into its ends through J from inside the cabinets. Both cabinets stand on open frames (I-E, J-E) attached with nails driven through the top of the bottom board (D).

The finish may be enamel applied over a prime coat.

FIND UNSUSPECTED STORAGE PLACES

A bit of imagination is an asset when you are faced with a need to add storage space in your house. Too often, we don't see any possibilities except the obvious.

Illustrated here are three ways to take advantage of such hidden assets. Look down and you'll find space at the bottom of closets. Look up and you'll find space on your garage ceiling. Look at wasted areas and you'll find unsuspected bonanzas, as in the kitchen cabinet idea shown in Fig. 5-16.

Aside from the immediate value of these ideas, let them also be a catalyst in opening your eyes to other possibilities.

Closet Floor

Bring order to the floor of your closet by building

Table 5-2. Materials for Storage Space on a Closet Floor.

A.	1″ × 6″ or 1″ × 8″ face
B.	1″ × 2″ cleat, size to fit closet
C.	1 pair small butt hinges
D.	1 lid, any 1/4″ or 1/2″ stock

this hinged-top box in which can be placed out-of-season bedding, footwear, rain boots, or just the clutter that seems to accumulate in clothes closets.

You'll want to use as much of the closet floor as possible, but the presence of the door frame will interfere. The face of the box should be placed as far forward as possible, butting against the inside edges of the frame.

Cut a piece of 1-×-6 or 1-×-8 stock wide enough to reach from one side of the closet to the other. (Table 5-2 and Fig. 5-13.) Stand it on edge

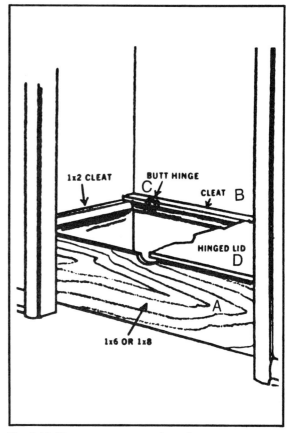

Fig. 5-13. Storage space on a closet floor.

against the inside of the doorway, then mark the side walls at the ends of this board. Nail small vertical cleats at these points, making them just as long as the board is high. Since you won't be able to nail to the cleats, glue the board instead. When the glue has dried, you can continue with the rest of the job. Nail two 1-×-2 cleats along the sides, leveling them with face. Nail another 1 × 2 across the back of the closet with its top edge higher than the other cleats by the thickness of the lid.

Attach small butt hinges to the lid and the back cleat. Cut a half-moon finger hole in the facing board. Paint with a tough gloss enamel to match the closet interior.

Garage Ceiling

If you don't want to go in for elaborate storage renovation schemes for your garage, good use can still be obtained from the top of your garage for storage of bulky items such as ladders, out-of-season storm windows or screens, lumber, and even fishing rods and skis.

**Table 5-3. Materials for
Storage Space in the Garage Ceiling.**

2 or more pairs steel shelf brackets
2 lengths 2″ × 3″ to suit
2″ #6 or #8 woodscrews and washers

Both systems illustrated in Figs. 5-14 and 5-15 are simple in the extreme. In Fig. 5-14, an extension ladder is supported at each end by two pairs of heavy steel angle brackets screwed together in a U (See also Table 5-3). One side of the U is fastened to the joist; the other is the support for the ladder. You just slide the ladder between the brackets. Surprisingly heavy loads can be carried in this manner.

Figure 5-15 differs in that the support comes from a piece of 2-×-3 stock placed between a pair of ordinary steel shelf brackets. (See Table 5-4.) Screws through the ends of the brackets hold the 2 × 3 in place. The result is a sort of open shelf whose width is determined by the length of the 2 × 3s. Similarly, the size of the bracket will decide the depth of the space.

The load-carrying capacity of either type of facility can be increased by adding sets of brackets at intermediate points.

Kitchen Sink Cabinet

Between the front of a sink and the face of the cabinet in which it is enclosed, is a wasted area the full width and depth of the basin. It is an ideal spot for clean-up materials—soaps, steel wool pads, cleansers, etc.—or even for a spice rack, as illustrated in Fig. 5-16.

You'll first want to see how much room you've got. Open the doors below and measure the space behind the dummy panel in front of the sink. If it's deep enough to store the things you want to put there—and it usually is—you'll need a saber saw to

Fig. 5-14. Storage space on a garage ceiling.

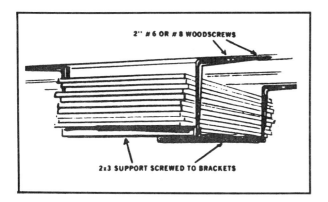

Fig. 5-15. Another example of storage space on the garage ceiling.

4 or more pairs heavy angle brackets
2" #6 or #8 woodscrews and washers

**Table 5-4. Materials for
Storage Space on the Garage Ceiling.**

cut it out. Draw guidelines and cut carefully. Sand the edges of both the opening and the panel you just cut out, then build a 1-×-2 platform with a retainer lip on the bottom of the panel. Test to be sure the new door will close flush. Trim the width of the platform if needed.

A pair of hinges that matches other kitchen hardware allows the door to open, and magnetic

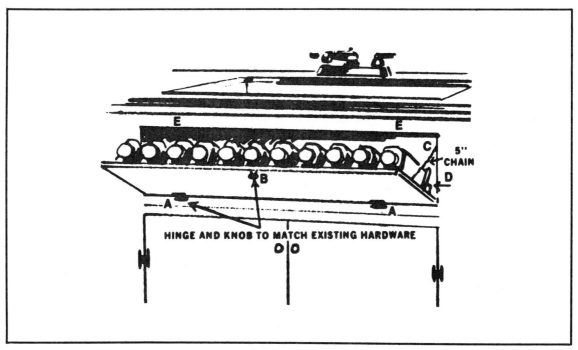

Fig. 5-16. Kitchen sink cabinet.

Table 5-5. Materials for Storage Space in the Kitchen Sink Cabinet.

A.	1 pair hinges, to match existing hardware
B.	1 matching knob
C.	5″ length of chain
D.	1″ × 2″ shelf cleat or metal spice rack
E.	1 pair magnetic latches

latches hold it shut, (Table 5-5.) Fasten a small piece of chain at one side to limit the movement of the door. Add a knob, seal the edges of the wood, and you've got a new hideaway.

You can save yourself the trouble of building a rack on the door if you can find a small one of the right size in your housewares store.

USE EMPTY WALLS FOR STORAGE

Good taste in design and simplicity of construction are the hallmarks of this two-piece project which creates attractive storage space on any open wall where none existed (Fig. 5-17). Despite its large capacity, it takes little room, and—circumstances permitting—could be made even larger by extensions on either or both sides in an L- or U-shaped configuration.

Refer to Table 5-6 for materials. The bookshelf half of the project was first built as a frame with mitered corners, but butt joints are equal acceptable. The sides were dadoed for the shelves, which in turn were given blind dadoes for the vertical dividers. Glue was applied to the side dadoes and the shelf edges, then the shelves were slid into place and clamped until the glue dried. Treat the verticals similarly. Built this way, the intermediate shelves (C) should measure 47 1/4 inches, allowing for dadoes 3/8 inch deep.

If blind dadoes for the vertical dividers are something you are not equipped to do, you can combine ordinary dadoes and butt nailing. Make a dado on the top surface of the upper intermediate shelf (C) and another dado on the underside of the lower intermediate shelf. These dadoes need be only 1/4 inch deep.

Now slide a vertical divider between the two intermediate shelves and drive finishing nails into the divider from above and below through both dadoes. The heads of the nails should be driven flush with the bottom surface of the dadoes.

The other dividers, above and below the one in the center, will each have a dado (and glue) to hold them on one edge and can be fastened at the other edge with finishing nails driven through the top and bottom (B), which are then set and filled.

An alternate method, without dadoes, would be to build the outer frame first, then glue and butt-nail shelves through the sides. The uprights between the intermediate shelves could then be glued and nailed from above and below. Lastly, the remaining uprights could be nailed through the top and bottom shelves and toenailed at the intermediate points. Either method applies to both cabinets; the only difference between them is that piano-hinged dropdown doors are fitted to the lower unit.

Where they reach adjoining walls, fasten the units by nailing through the sides into wall studs. When they must be supported by the wall on which they hang, cleats nailed to wall studs will carry the bulk of the load, and L-brackets at the tops will finish the job. Cleats can be concealed inside the cabinet by the doors but you may not want to use them under the bookshelves where they might be noticed. In that case, use big, 6-inch L-brackets at the bottom and at the top, concealing the vertical legs behind the dividers (D) and the ends (A). Use No. 8 3-inch flat-head screws to fasten the L-brackets to the studs. If the dividers do not coincide with studs, place the upper brackets under the top (B) and fasten them to the studs wherever you can find them. Paint the exposed leg the same color as the wall and rely on books to conceal them.

Treat the lower brackets the same way but be sure that the horizontal legs are placed *under* the bottom shelf (B). You may have to notch the back edge of the shelf slightly to accommodate the thickness of the vertical legs if you want to keep the bookcase tight against the wall.

When it comes to finishing, much depends on whether you want a paint or a clear finish. In any case, sand thoroughly with successively finer

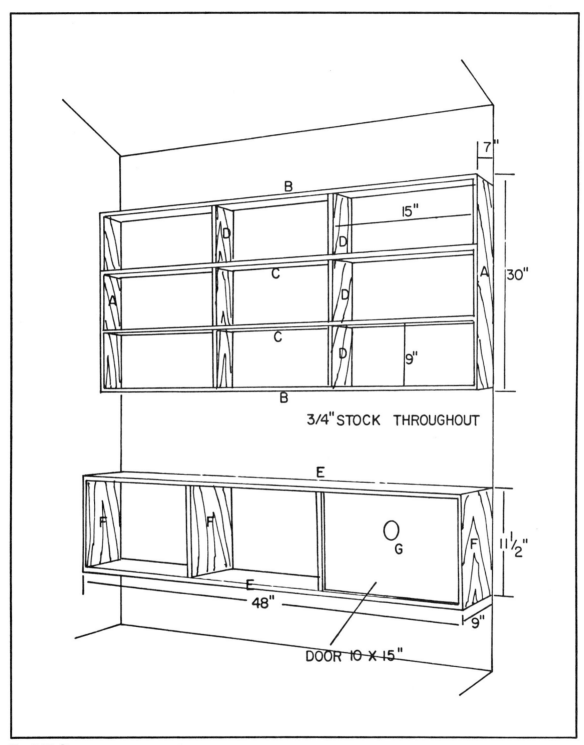

Fig. 5-17. Storage on an empty wall.

Table 5-6. Materials for the Bookshelf.

A.	2 pcs,	3/4″ × 7″ × 30″
B.	2 pcs,	3/4″ × 7″ × 48″
C.	2 pcs,	3/4″ × 7″ × 46 1/2″
D.	6 pcs,	3/4″ × 7″ × 9″
E.	2 pcs,	3/4″ × 9″ × 48″
F.	4 pcs,	3/4″ × 10″ × 9″
G.	3 pcs,	3/4″ × 10″ × 15″

aluminum-oxide open-coat paper. For a paint finish, you can use an orbital sander that operates at about 3000 orbits per minute since the slight swirl marks will not show under an opaque coating.

If, however, you are going to stain and use a clear finish, use either a fast sander that operates at 10,000 orbits per minute or a slow dual-action sander which permits you to follow up orbital with straight-line sanding. In this way you can eliminate the swirl marks which staining will accentuate.

For a paint finish, apply a coat of primer which is then lightly sanded with 120-grit sandpaper. Follow with two coats of enamel of the semi-gloss type.

A clear finish will require a coat of well-wiped stain to avoid streaking, followed by two coats of lacquer, varnish, or clear urethane. You might be interested in a clear finish called *Zar,* which combines phenolic resin and tung oil and is wiped on, rather than brushed. All of these clear coatings should be rubbed with very fine steel wool between coats as well as the final coat.

MAKE A HANDY CABINET/TOWEL RACK

A convenient cabinet/towel rack combination can easily be recessed into a new wall or, with a little more effort, into an existing wall (Fig. 5-18).

In a wall with studs 16 inches on center, a section of one stud is removed so the preassembled unit can be placed in the space. Two by fours are installed above and below the area (Fig. 5-19).

Total width of the unit is 30 inches, but the height can vary according to the size shutter obtained for the cabinet door. In the example, the shutter is 49 1/2 inches deep by 13 1/2 inches wide, which leaves ample space to install two towel bars.

Material for the project includes 1-×-6 and 1-×-4 lumber, 1/2-inch plywood for the adjustable shelves, 1/2-inch doweling, 3/4-inch aluminum tubing, a pair of hinges (offset style for surface mounting shutter), a magnetic catch, a shutter, and a knob (Table 5-7). Backing material such as 1/8-inch hardboard may be needed if the inside of the wall that is exposed can't be used.

Three sides of the unit are made of 1-×-6 material, with the top and bottom pieces notched for the shutter, as shown in Fig. 5-19. Before putting the upright 1 × 4s in place, drill 1/2-inch holes 1/2 inch deep in both pieces in the pattern illustrated so you can insert the pegs to support the adjustable shelves. (An optional approach is to install metal brackets available for adjustable shelves.)

For the towel bars, cut two lengths of 3/4-inch aluminum tubing. In the 1 × 6 at the right, drill holes for short lengths of 1/2-inch doweling. Also glue dowel plugs in one end of each tube. Then glue the right end of each tube over the dowel stub, and fasten the other end with a screw through the center upright into the plug.

Shelf pegs are made of 1/2-inch doweling. Each is 1 inch long, with a quarter section cut out. The shelf fits in the cutout area when in place and locks the peg in position. Here too, metal shelf supports can be used.

After the unit is nailed in place, fill wall joints and nail holes as necessary and paint to suit room decor. The example is painted with latex semi-gloss like the wall, with the shutter a contrasting color.

BUILD IN HIS AND HER CLOSETS

How do you provide enough space to hang clothes and ample drawer space suitable for a man and a woman that can be quickly hidden away? By building this closet that contains 14 drawers and 4 separate clothes hanging sections which can be quickly hidden by folding doors (Fig. 5-20). This project saves on floor space as well—space that is normally used by bureau drawers.

Refer to Fig. 5-21 and Table 5-8. While there is no particular way to start this project, most of whose construction is obvious, it is suggested that you start by securing the cross rail (L) to the wall studs and the drawer section supports (B) to the floor. A few construction details, however, should be pointed out.

At the top of the closet, the piece across the front (P) is end-lapped with the side piece (O). Pieces between the drawers (G) are dadoed into the upright pieces (F). The drawer slides (I) are dadoed into the upright frame (C), and fit into grooves on the sides of the drawers that measure 1/4 inch deep by 1 1/8 inch high. The drawers themselves are grooved with 1/4-inch dadoes in their fronts, backs, and sides to receive the bottoms. No drawer stops are necessary because the 1/2-inch overlaps on the top of the drawers effectively serve as the drawer stops.

As was mentioned previously, one of the nice things about this closet is that it can be quickly hidden by the sliding doors (Y). Each of these doors comes in two parts to make it easy to get to the inside of the closet without having to open any one door completely. There is no reason to buy

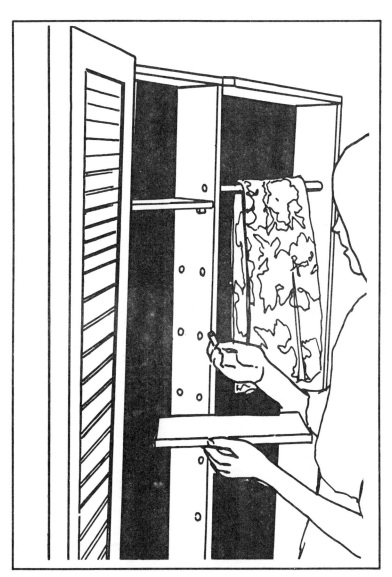

Fig. 5-18. Handy Cabinet/Towel Rack.

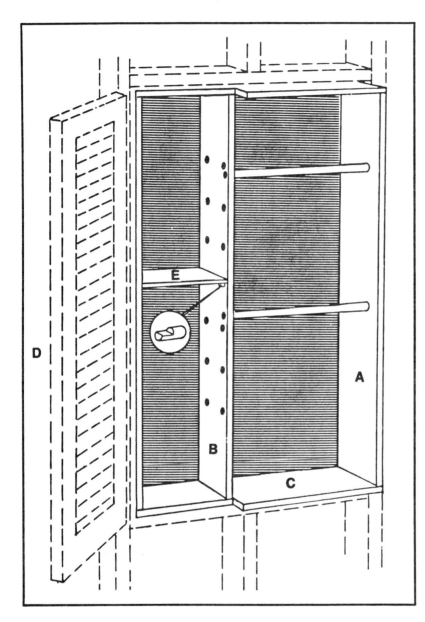

Fig. 5-19. Details for the Handy Cabinet/Towel Rack.

furniture-grade lumber for this project since just about everything is to be painted to complement the decor of the room.

MAKE A MODERNISTIC BUREAU

Here's a project that looks very modernistic and boxy but has a simple, handsome appearance (Fig. 5-22). Although it seems complex, it is actually very easy to put together with butt joints fastened with white glue and 2-inch finishing nails.

Refer to Table 5-9 and Fig. 5-23. The top and bottom (C) are single pieces of 3/4-inch plywood cut from one 4- × -8-foot sheet. The end pieces and the two intervening verticals (D) are all the same size and are cut from one sheet of plywood. All 11 drawer fronts (A and B) can also be conveniently cut from this same sheet.

Table 5-7. Materials for the Handy Cabinet/Towel Rack.

A.	1 pc, 3/4″ × 6″ × 48″
B.	2 pcs, 3/4″ × 4 1/4″ × 48″
C.	2 pcs, 3/4″ × 6″ × 30″
D.	1 pc, 1 3/4″ × 13 1/2″ × 49 1/2″ shutter
E.	2 pcs, 1/2″ × 12″ × 4 1/4″

2 offset hinges
shutter knob

The back (E) is also a single sheet of 3/4-inch plywood and is anchored to the wall behind it with six 1/4-inch lag screws and washers. The lag screws are 4 inches long and are driven into predrilled holes through the plasterboard and studs.

The tall, narrow bookcases are essentially decorative and can be used for books and small ornaments. These bookcases and their shelves are made of 3/4-inch lumber or plywood. The shelves can be adjustable or fixed. Fixed shelves will make the cases stronger and will require only a 1/4-inch

back. The shelves can be fastened with glue and finishing nails driven through the sides and into the edges of the shelves. If you prefer adjustable shelves, make the back 1/2-inch thick.

The right-hand bookcase is fastened to the top surface of the bureau with glue and 1 1/4-inch No. 8 screws driven from below. The top of the case is fastened to the wall behind it with screws and angle braces.

Fastening the left-hand case is done in the same way: angle braces at the top to the wall behind, and No. 8 screws driven through the left side of the bureau. The door (F) on this bookcase is optional.

The finish in this instance is two coats of white alkyd enamel over a white primer. Of course, the color depends on your own particular decorative scheme, as do glass drawer knobs.

MAKE THE MOST OF UNDER-STAIRS SPACE

If you've been wondering what to do with that wasted space beneath your staircase, why not convert it into an efficient storage area? This transfor-

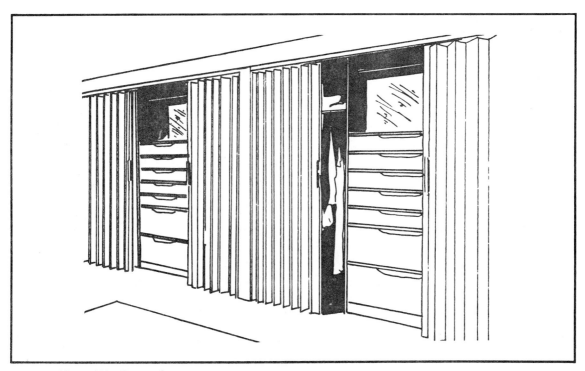

Fig. 5-20. His and Her Built-In Closets.

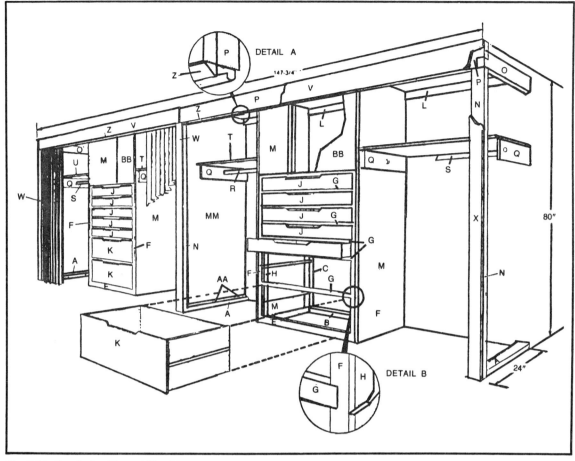

Fig. 5-21. Details for His and Her Closets.

mation an easily be made by constructing a series of rolling shelf compartments, which maximizes the available space and makes all the contents available without stretching (Fig. 5-24).

If you are presently building a new staircase, now would be an ideal opportunity to install the compartments. If however, you plan to build them into your present staircase, you can do so without much difficulty.

Refer to Fig. 5-25 and Table 5-10. In either case, you must start by building a framework which serves to separate the compartments, as well as giving extra support to the steps (Fig. 5-26). The framework, made up of 2-×-3 studding on 16-inch centers, divides the space into five sections. In order to secure the bottom plates (frame horizontals)

to the floor, drive countersunk #10 wood screws through the plates into the floor. Before gluing and screwing the framework to the stairjacks, the tops of the framework must be rabbeted to ensure a snug fit.

Too narrow for an additional compartment, the last section is ideal for a small closet. To build the closet, simply line the inside of the framework with the same type of paneling which will be used to cover the outside of the entire unit. After hanging the door and attaching the necessary molding, the closet will be complete. Although the closet is shallow, the addition of adjustable shelves will make it quite useful. You may, however, wish to close off the last section with paneling, thus eliminating the closet.

Table 5-8. Materials for His and Her Closets.

A.	3 pcs, each: 21″ × 4″ × 2″	N.	3 pcs, each: 74″ × 4″ × 2″ (1 not shown)
B.	4 pcs, each: 20″ × 2″ × 2″ (1 not shown)	O.	2 pcs, each: 23″ × 4″ × 3″
C.	4 pcs, each: 56″ × 2″ × 2″ (3 not shown)	P.	1 pc, 147 3/4″ × 6″ × 2″
D.	8 pcs, each: 21″ × 2″ × 2″ (7 not shown)	Q.	8 pcs, each: 20″ × 6″ × 1″ (3 not shown)
E.	2 pcs, each: 20″ × 4″ × 2″	R.	2 pcs, each: 24″ × 1 1/2″ (dia.)(1 not shown)
F.	4 pcs, each: 57″ × 2″ × 1″	S.	2 pcs, each: 23 1/4″ × 1 1/2″ (dia.)
G.	14 pcs, each: 21″ × 2″ × 1″	T.	2 pcs, each: 24″ × 20″ × 1″
H.	4 pcs, each: 57″ × 2″ × 2″ (2 not shown)	U.	2 pcs, each: 23 1/4″ × 20″ × 1″
I.	28 pcs, each: 20″ × 1″ × 1″ (18 not shown)	V.	2 pcs, each: 73 7/8″ × 6″ × 1″
		W.	2 pcs, each: 74″ × 4″ × 1″
J.	10 drawers, each: 1 front, 19 7/8″ × 4 1/2″ × 3/4″; 2 sides, 22 1/8″ × 4″ × 1/2″; 1 back, 20 3/8″ × 4″ × 1/2″; 1 bottom, 21 1/8″ × 20 3/8″ × 1/4″	X.	1 pc, 74″ × 5″ × 1″
		Y.	2 folding doors, each: 73 7/8″ × 74″ (1 not shown)
		Z.	2 moldings, each: 73 7/8″
K.	4 drawers, each: 1 front, 19 7/8″ × 10 1/2″ × 3/4″; 2 sides, 22 1/8″ × 10″ × 1/2″; 1 back, 20 7/8″ × 10″ × 1/2″; 1 bottom, 21 1/8″ × 20 3/8″ × 1/4″ (1 not shown)	AA.	2 1/4-round moldings, each: 21″ (1 not shown)
		BB.	2 mirrors, each: 21″ × 19″
		CC.	2 1/4-round moldings, each: 22″ (not shown)
		DD.	2 1/4-round moldings, each: 20″ (not shown)
L.	1 pc, 143 3/4″ × 4″ × 2″	EE.	2 fluorescent lamps, each: 21″ (not shown)
M.	5 pcs, each: 80″ × 24″ × 3/4″ (1 not shown)	MM.	1 pc, 80″ × 21″ × 3/4″

Fig. 5-22. A Modernistic Bureau.

Table 5-9. Materials for the Modernistic Bureau.

A. 8 pcs, 3/4" × 5" × 20"
B. 3 pcs, 3/4" × 6 11/16" × 30"
C. 2 pcs, 3/4" × 18 3/4" × 73 3/8"
D. 4 pcs, 3/4" × 18" × 20 5/16"
E. 1 pc, 3/4" × 20 5/16" × 73 3/8"
F. 1 pc, 3/4" × 10" × 25 1/2"
G. 1 pc, 1/4" × 11 1/2" × 78"
H. 3 pcs, 3/4" × 10" × 11 1/2"
I. 7 pcs, 3/4" × 10" × 10"
J. 2 pcs, 3/4" × 10" × 77 1/4"
K. 2 pcs, 3/4" × 3/4" × 3/4"
L. 1 pc, 3/4" × 5" × 10"

M. 2 pcs, 3/4" × 10" × 62 1/2"
N. 1 pc, 1/4" × 11 1/2" × 64"
O. 3 pcs, 1/4" × 16" × 28"
P. 6 pcs, 1/2" × 5 3/4" × 16"
Q. 3 pcs, 1/2" × 5 3/4" × 27 1/2"
R. 22 pcs, 3/4" × 3/4" × 16"
S. 16 pcs, 1/2" × 4 1/4" × 16"
T. 8 pcs, 1/2" × 4 1/4" × 17 1/2"
U. 8 pcs, 1/4" × 16" × 18"
V. 44 pcs, 3/4" × 3/4" × 17 1/4"
W. 20 pcs, "L-bracket" shelf supports
X. 2 pcs, pivot hinges
Y. 1 pc, 3/4" × 1 1/2" × 73 3/8"

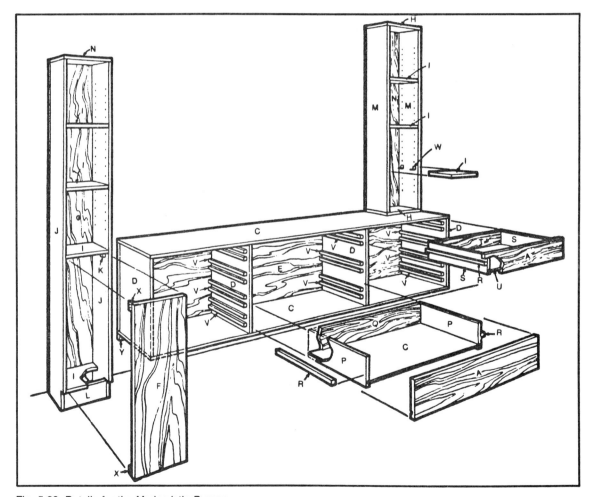

Fig. 5-23. Details for the Modernistic Bureau.

110

Fig. 5-24. View of the finished under-stairs cabinets shows that accessibility is their most attractive feature.

The construction of the four shelf compartments is fairly simple. Each compartment is 14 1/4 inches wide and 36 1/2 inches long, in order to fit loosely within the framework. Since most staircases vary in size, slight modifications of this plan may be necessary. The height of each compartment will vary according to its position, and the angle of the tops of the compartments will depend on the angle of the staircase.

The shelves and end pieces are built of 3/4-inch fir plywood, butted and fastened with glue and screws. The back, a solid sheet of 1/4-inch plywood, is glued and nailed with finishing nails to the back edges of the end pieces and shelves. The shelves are simply nailed through the sides and back and glued in simple butt joints. To conceal the rubber rollers (nonswiveling casters), extend the back and

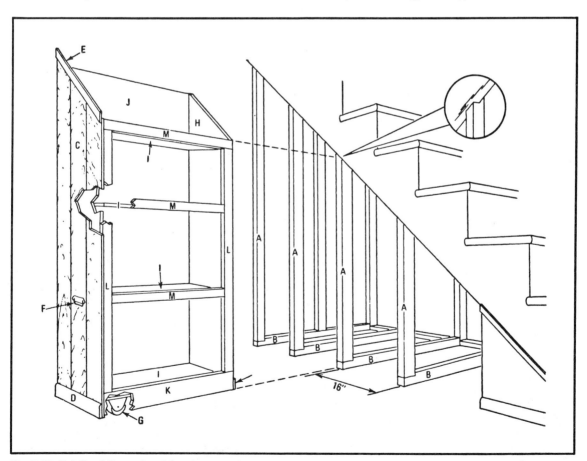

Fig. 5-25. Details of the under-stairs storage space.

Table 5-10. Materials for the Under-Stairs Storage Compartments.

A. 1 1/2" × 2 1/2", height to suit
B. 1 1/2" × 2 1/2" × 36 1/2"
C. 1/4" × 16", height to suit
D. 1/2" × 3" × 16"
E. trim molding
F. handles
G. 20 non-swiveling casters (4 for each compartment)
H. 3/4" × 13 1/4", height to suit
I. 3/4" × 13 1/4" × 34 1/4"
J. 1/4" × 35 3/4", height to suit
K. 3/4" × 6" × 35 3/4"
L. 3/4" × 1 1/2", height to suit
M. 3/4" × 1 1/2" × 32 3/4"
N. 1/2" × 14 1/4" × 4"

end pieces down a few inches beyond the bottom shelf. Allow a 1/4-inch clearance for the bottom piece.

Ledge molding of 3/4-×-1 1/2-inch pine is then glued and nailed to the front of the compartments in order to conceal the plywood edges. The molding also gives added support and is useful for keeping the contents of the shelves from falling out. The bottom piece on each compartment should extend below the lowest shelf as far as the end and back pieces to help conceal the rollers.

The rubber rollers secured to the bottom of each compartment allow the compartments to roll freely, making their contents accessible to the smallest child.

In order to conceal the compartments, paneling must be fastened to the face of each compartment (Fig. 5-27). Use paneling cement and a few panel nails with colored heads to fasten the paneling in place. Note that the paneling (E) on the front end of each compartment is 16 inches wide and thus overlaps the studs (A) that divide these rolling shelves from each other. Take special care to cut the paneling correctly so that when the unit is closed, the wall will appear to be in one piece. Next, attach molding and handles.

Finish the project by sanding the interior parts and apply two coats of shellac and one of varnish.

USE A PLANTER/CABINET AS A ROOM SEPARATOR

A planter which also serves as a cabinet and room separator can be both highly decorative and practical. The design in Fig. 5-28 which was created by the editors of Family Handyman, easily and handsomely fulfills all three functions.

The design was submitted to Bernard Gladstone, a well-known writer on home-improvement subjects, who built the planter in his

Fig. 5-26. Dividers made of 2 × 3s keep the cabinets in line for smoother rolling in and out.

Fig. 5-27. Carefully matched molding and paneling make roll-out cabinet joints invisible.

Fig. 5-28. Planter/Cabinet.

well-equipped workshop. All of the exterior parts are made of teak-veneered 3/4-inch plywood. Of course, your own copy of this piece need not be teak-veneered. Teak, birch, walnut, or any other suitable furniture veneer or even painted plywood can be used, depending on the decor of your rooms.

Some parts, such as the mitered joints where the sides (D) and ends (E) meet, can be cut on a bench or radial arm saw. (See Fig. 5-29 and Table 5-11.) If you don't have either of these tools, have these parts cut by a professional carpenter or cabinetmaker. A portable electric circular saw turned to 45 degrees or a powerful portable saber saw, however, can easily make the bevels required for miter joints.

Both sides of the planter are identical, since in this case it was used to separate a living room from a dining room. Therefore, both sides have exactly the same kind of doors so that access to the con-

tents of the cabinet is possible from the dining or living room.

The sides (D) are cut from one piece of plywood; the doors (E) are also cut in one piece to preserve the continuity of the veneer grain (Fig. 5-30). The method of cutting the doors is very interesting. After marking the width and the combined length of both doors on the face of the side (D), a wooden straightedge was clamped to the side, and a portable circular power saw with a fine-toothed blade was placed against the edge in a plunge cut and run along the marked line almost to its end (Fig. 5-31). This procedure was repeated on the remaining marked lines of the door. The corner ends were completed with a portable saber saw and filed to make the width of the cuts from two different kinds of blades identical.

The door panel was then lifted out of the larger sheet (D) and cut in halves to form the two doors

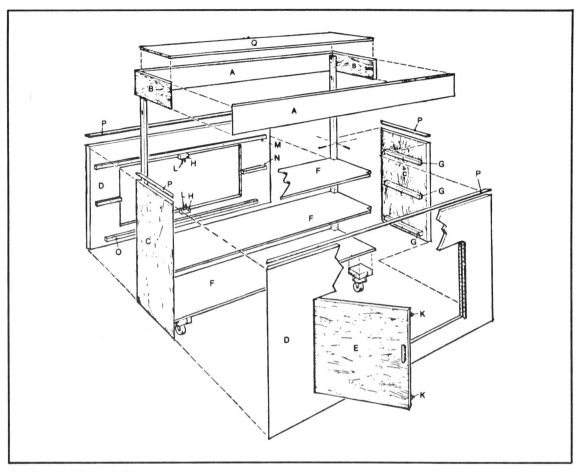

Fig. 5-29. Details of the Planter/Cabinet.

(E,E) (Fig. 5-32). You don't have to have a portable circular or table saw to perform this operation; it can also be done with a good portable jigsaw or saber saw.

The sides have three cleats, (O, N, M) fastened with glue and screws to support the front and back edges of the three shelves inside. The shelves are smoothly sanded 1/2-inch plywood. The ends of the

Table 5-11. Materials for the Planter/Cabinet.

A.	2 pcs, 3/4″ × 5 3/4″ × 72″		J.	4 pcs, 4″ × 4″ × thickness to suit
B.	2 pcs, 3/4″ × 5 3/8″ × 21″			
C.	2 pcs, 3/4″ × 21″ × 36″		K.	4 engages for rollers
D.	2 pcs, 3/4″ × 21″ × 72″		L.	4 nylon roller catches
E.	4 pcs, 3/4″ × 26″ × 21″		M.	2 pcs, 1″ × 1″ × 68 3/8″
F.	3 pcs, 1/2″ × 19 1/2″ × 70 1/2″		N.	4 pcs, 1″ × 1″ × 8″
G.	6 pcs, 1″ × 1″ × 17 3/8″		O.	2 pcs, 1″ × 1″ × 62 3/8″
H.	4 pcs, 1 3/4″ × 1 3/4″ × 4″		P.	16 feet of 3/4″ veneer tape
I.	4 pcs, 1″ × 1″ × 61″		Q.	1 pc, 3/4″ × 19 1/2″ × 70 1/2″

114

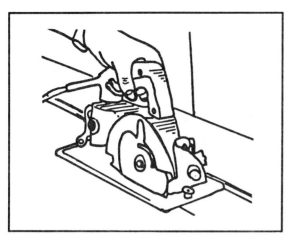

Fig. 5-30. To preserve the continuity of the veneer grain, two doors and one side are cut from one piece of plywood.

Fig. 5-32. A cleanly cut panel from which two doors will be made is lifted from the larger side piece. A saber saw used to square the corner cuts. Unevenness was smoothed by filing.

shelves are supported by cleats (G) screwed and glued to the inner sides of the ends (C). All four doors swing on continuous hinges because they are so wide (Fig. 5-33).

The corner joints where the sides (D) and ends (C) meet are mitered. These joints were fastened with glue and held in clamps overnight (Fig. 5-34). If you use plain plywood that will be covered with a paint finish, you can join the sides and ends with simple butt joints fastened with glue and finishing nails and then fill the nail holes with water putty. The middle and upper shelves (F) are both notched at the corners to permit the four chrome, 1-inch-square tubing supports that hold up the "roof" of the planter to pass through (Figs. 5-35 and 5-36). The lower ends of these tubes rest on the bottom shelf.

Each piece of square tubing has 8 pairs of holes

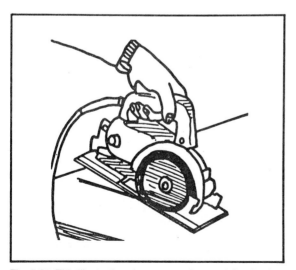

Fig. 5-31. This illustration shows a wooden straightedge being used as a guide for accurate plunge-cutting of the door panels.

Fig. 5-33. Flush-fit doors are mounted to the side pieces with piano-type hinges.

115

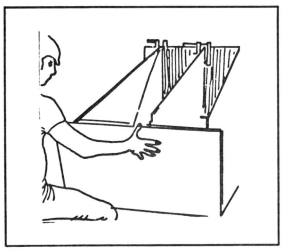

Fig. 5-34. End pieces are fitted to the partially assembled frame, with shelves clamped temporarily for gluing.

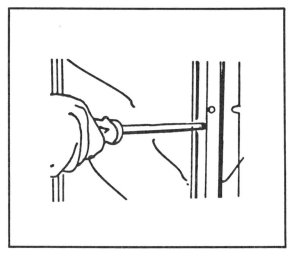

Fig. 5-36. With the main planter box assembled, the chrome, 1-inch-square tubing supports which hold up the roof of the planter are passed through the notched shelf corners and screwed to the sides.

drilled through it for roundhead screws. There are 2 pairs above each shelf (in every corner on the inside) and two pairs in each corner where the tubing supports the roof (Fig. 5-37). The pairs of holes are slightly offset so that you can drive screws through the tubing into the end pieces (C) and also into the sides (D). Do the same to the roof where the screws are driven into the ends (B) and sides (A) in each corner. This procedure not only anchors the tubing but braces all the corners firmly.

The top of the planter has a recess in it that is 5 3/4 inches deep. The upper shelf (F) forms the bottom of this recess. The recess is designed to contain a pan made of sheet metal with well-soldered joints so that it will not leak (Fig. 5-38). It should be filled with small gravel on which flowerpots for houseplants can be placed.

The roof or light box supported by the four square tubes is assembled with the same kind of glued mitered joints as the cabinet. The upper

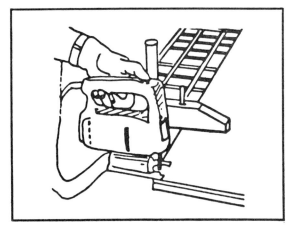

Fig. 5-35. Corner-notching of the middle and upper shelves is easily done with a saber saw. Notches accommodate the tubing supports.

Fig. 5-37. The planter roof or light box is placed on the four tubing supports and fastened by driving a pair of roundhead wood screws into the side pieces at each of the corners.

Fig. 5-38. This view of the planter shows the 5 3/4-inch recess that will hold the soldered sheet metal pan. Actually the upper shelf forms the bottom of this recess. Note the offset holes in the square tubing. Each tubing section has eight pairs of these holes.

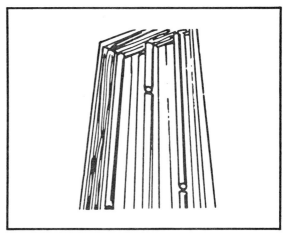

Fig. 5-39. The planter roof is also a light box that supports three rows of 40- and 20-watt fluorescent lamp fixtures.

edges of the roof sides (A) and ends (B) enclose and are flush with a sheet of plain, well-sanded plywood (Q) which is glued into place.

The underside of the light box or roof has three rows of fluorescent lights, each row made up of a 40- and a 20-watt lamp (Fig. 5-39). One of the corner square tubes has a large enough hole in it at the top so that the electric cable for the fluorescent lamps can be passed down through the tube to a

hole in the bottom of the cabinet and out to an electrical outlet (Fig. 5-40).

Strips of matching veneer tape go all around the top of the recess to provide this top edge and exposed low edges of A and B with a finished look.

The underside of the bottom shelf (L) has four swiveling casters mounted on wood blocks deep enough to allow a 3/8-inch clearance between the bottom of the cabinet and the floor (Fig. 5-41).

The finish depends on the material you have used. If it is plywood with a hardwood veneer, use

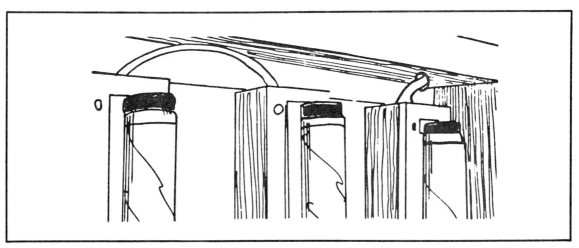

Fig. 5-40. The view from the underside of the finished planter roof shows the fluorescent fixtures wired in place. Note the access hole filed in the upper end of the support tubing. The fixtures are wired in parallel, and the power cable runs down through the tube and out the cabinet bottom to the outlet.

Fig. 5-41. Four swiveling casters are mounted on wood blocks, which in turn are fastened to the underside of the bottom cabinet shelf.

an appropriate stain and finish with clear lacquer, urethane, or standard varnish. In this particular case, the plain plywood top and shelves were stained to match the teak, and the entire assembly was treated with a penetrating finish, rubbed with very fine steel wool, and waxed.

Chapter 6

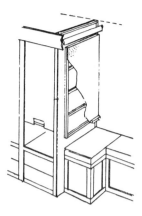

Hobby Projects

If your wife can sew, she'd really appreciate one of the sewing projects given in this chapter so she wouldn't continually have to find a place to store her projects. The children will love the handy alcove for the basement playroom, too. Space for hobbies is as important as any other home project, and the ideas in this chapter should help you provide room for all of them.

PROVIDE A BUILT-IN SEWING CENTER

If you have a corner of a room that is not being utilized, transform it into a storage complex of shelves and drawers for sewing materials by constructing this attractive built-in sewing center (Fig. 6-1). The center, which is less than 3 feet wide, will provide ample space for the orderly accumulation of various materials and implements used in sewing.

The project is made almost completely of 3/4-inch plywood (Table 6-1 and Fig. 6-2). The existing plasterboard wall forms the back of the center. Butt joints are used, and are secured with glue

and finishing nails. You may wish to buy a ready-made chest of drawers for the bottom portion of the center and build the remaining structure, or you may want to do the entire construction yourself. The top (B) is anchored securely to the wall with two 3-inch, right-angle braces (not included in Table 6-1) fastened with screws.

The back of the vertical compartment (L) is 1/8-inch perforated hardboard made with holes spaced in 1-inch-square patterns for the insertion of hooks. This hardboard is fastened to a cove molding frame (N), which is slightly forward from the rear wall to allow room for the ends of hooks. Both sliding doors (K) (only one is shown) are decorative-type 1/8-inch perforated hardboard. These doors slide in either wood, metal, or plastic tracks, which can be purchased in many hardware or building supply stores. The bottom shelf (E) in the middle section is attached to the top (B) of the drawer section by screws through the bottom of B. The screws are driven flush to avoid snags when using the center's top drawer.

The drawers are standard construction. The

Fig. 6-1. The built-in Sewing Center.

Table 6-1. Materials for the Built-In Sewing Center.

A.	2 pcs, 20″ × 8′ × 3/4″	Q.	4 pcs, 7 3/8″ × 18 3/4″ × 1/2″
B.	8 pcs, 20″ × 30″ × 3/4″	R.	2 pcs, 7 3/8″ × 27 7/16″ × 1/2″
C.	1 pc, 19″ × 30″ × 3/4″	S.	4 pcs, 3 3/8″ × 18 3/4″ × 1/2″
D.	2 pcs, wood, metal or plastic track, 30″ each	T.	2 pcs, 3 3/8″ × 27 7/16″ × 1/2″
		U.	4 pcs, 18 3/4″ × 27 15/16″ × 1/4″
E.	4 pcs, 20″ × 20″ × 3/4″	V.	10 pcs, 1″ × 3″ × 9 3/4″
F.	1 pc, 20″ × 28″ × 3/4″	W.	4 pcs, 1″ × 3″ × 63 3/4″
G.	8 pcs, 1/2″ × 1/2″ × 1″	X.	2 pcs, 9 3/4″ × 8 1/2″ × 1/8″ (top)
H.	1 pc, 1 1/2″ × 25 1/2″ × 3/4″		2 pcs, 9 3/4″ × 24 3/4″ × 1/8″ (bottom)
I.	1 pc, 1 1/2″ × 31 1/2″ × 1″		2 pcs, 9 3/4″ × 30 3/4″ × 1/8″ (middle)
J.	2 pcs, 2 1/2″ × 30″ × 3/4″		
K.	2 pcs, 16″ × 23 1/2″ × 1/8″		
L.	1 pc, 9 1/4″ × 28″ × 1/8″	Y.	38 ft. of 1/4″ × 5/8″ beading
M.	8 pcs, 1/2″ × 1/2″ × 19 1/4″	Z.	38 ft. of 1/4″ × 5/8″ molding
N.	9 1/4″ × 28″ × 3/4″		Not shown: 4 pcs, 1″ × 3″ × 14 1/4″ (top door vertical frames)
O.	2 pcs, 7 3/8″ × 28 7/16″ × 3/4″		
P.	2 pcs, 3 3/8″ × 28 7/16″ × 3/4″		

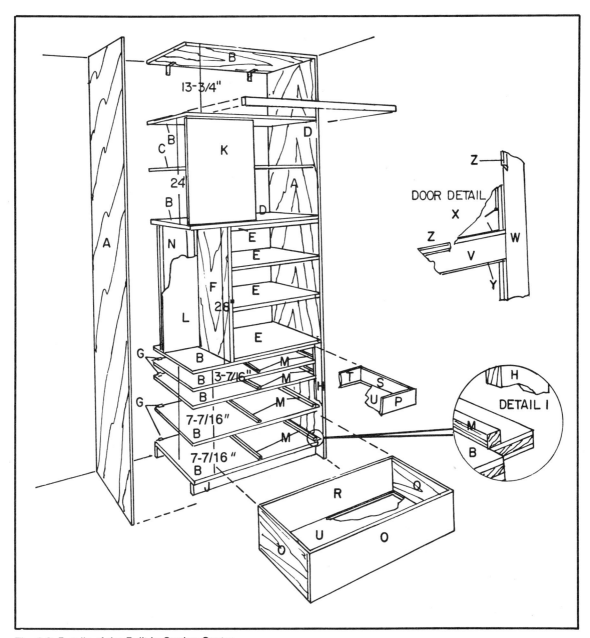

Fig. 6-2. Details of the Built-In Sewing Center.

sides (Q,S), backs (R,T), and fronts (O,P) are grooved to receive the hardboard bottoms (U). The notch on the back of the drawer (R) is for the center drawer guide (M). A 1 1/2-inch wide, vertical strip (H) covers the ends of the drawer guides (M) on the right and allows the drawers to be pulled out

freely without interference from the bottom bifold door when it is open. The drawers are flush with the sides (A) of the center.

Each of the bifold doors, both upper and lower, have two continuous piano-type hinges. To allow the doors to close fully and still leave room for the drawer knobs, the doors have panels (X) flush with the sides (W), and crossbars (V) on the front of the door frame, but no panels on the backside, as shown in the Door Detail, thus leaving a recessed area for clearance. The door frame is made of 1 × 3s; the 1-inch thickness is an actual measurement (as are all the measurements in this project) to allow enough clearance for drawer knobs that protrude 3/4 inch.

MAKE A SEWING CLOSET

Here's a sewing closet to inspire the seamstress in

any woman (Fig. 6-3). Behind the double bifold doors are shelves for material storage; drawers to hold thread, scissors, and other gadgets; a compartment for the sewing machine; and a stand-up cubby for the ironing board. You can build it in practically any room of the house.

Refer to Fig. 6-4 and Table 6-2. The floor and ceiling frames (Q,R) are nailed in place after the base, shoe, and cove moldings have been cut away to allow rear frame pieces (Q) a flush fit against the wall at the ceiling and floor. The upper front frame piece (Q) will support the track for the folding

Fig. 6-3. The Sewing Closet.

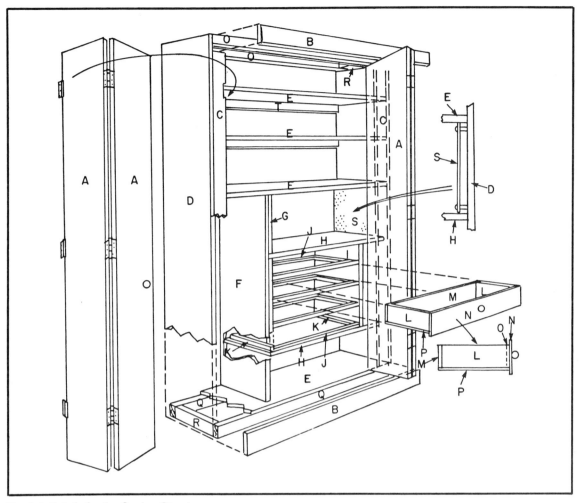

Fig. 6-4. Details for the Sewing Closet.

Table 6-2. Materials for the Sewing Closet.

A.	4 pcs, 3/4" × 9 1/4" × 88 7/8"		L.	8 pcs, 3/8" × 3 1/4" × 13"
B.	2 pcs, 3/4" × 3 1/2" × 37"		M.	4 pcs, 3/8" × 3 1/4" × 21 15/16"
C.	2 pcs, 3/4" × 3 1/2" × 96"		N.	4 pcs, 1/4" × 4" × 22 1/2"
D.	2 pcs, 3/4" × 16" × 96"		O.	4 pcs, 1/4" × 3 1/4" × 21 1/8"
E.	4 pcs, 3/4" × 16" × 42 1/2"		P.	4 pcs, 1/4" × 13 3/8" × 21 15/16"
F.	1 pc, 3/4" × 14" × 60"		Q.	4 pcs, 1 1/2" × 2 1/2" × 42 1/2"
G.	1 pc, 3/4" × 14" × 24"		R.	4 pcs, 1 1/2" × 2 1/2" × 13"
H.	2 pcs, 3/4" × 14" × 28"		S.	1 pc, 1/4" × 14" × 24"
I.	2 pcs, 3/4" × 14" × 18"		T.	2 pcs, 3/4" × 1 1/2" × 42 1/2"
J.	5 pcs, 3/4" × 3/4" × 22"		U.	12 hinges, 1 1/2" × 2"
K.	8 pcs, 3/4" × 3/4" × 13 1/2"		V.	bifold track hardware

doors. Next, cleats (T), which give added support to the upper shelves (E), are nailed to the wall studs.

Before you nail on plywood side panels (D), the floor shelf (E) should be fastened to the floor frame. The remaining three main shelves (E) are then positioned and glued, and 1 1/2-inch finishing nails driven into them through the side panels on both sides. A level should be used to ensure straightness of the shelves.

The vertical closet divider (F) is 28 inches from the right side panel. Finishing nails are driven into it through the top of the shelf above it (E). At the bottom, F is toenailed. These inside panel pieces are all cut from 3/4-inch cabinet-grade plywood.

Next, the two compartment panels (H) are positioned and secured with glue, and 1 1/2-inch finishing nails are driven through F and through the right side panel. With vertical pieces (I) nailed in place next, the drawer compartment is enclosed all around. Finally, the support panel (G) is fastened with nails and glue to F, E, and H.

The 3/4- × -3/4-inch drawer and guide supports (J,K) are nailed and glued inside of the drawer compartment. Careful attention must be paid to proper spacing so that the drawers will not stick later. Note that the height of each of the four spaces created by installing the drawer guide supports is 3 9/16 inches, while the drawers are only 3 1/2 inches high.

The four drawer bottoms (P) are cut from 1/4-inch hardboard, while the drawer sides (L) and backs (M) are 3/8-inch plywood. The drawer fronts (N,0) are formed by gluing together two pieces of 1/4-inch cabinet-grade plywood, which gives a better gluing edge in front for the drawer bottoms and sides and eliminates the need for routing a special groove. When gluing N and O together, the smaller rear piece should be centered side to side and positioned 1/4 inch from the top edge of N.

All of the drawer pieces are butt-jointed and secured with 1-inch brads and glue. The slight bevel on the front edges of the drawers can be produced either by planing or by sanding. The round wooden drawer pulls are available in hardware and lumber supply stores.

The 1- × -4-inch door frame pieces (B,C) are nailed to the closet assembly before the doors are hung. The hinge mortises are cut 3/4 inch wide, 1/8 inch deep, and 2 inches long using a sharp wood chisel. As mentioned, the folding door track is fastened to the upper front ceiling frame piece (Q) with shims between the two, if necessary to achieve the proper hanging height.

The 1/8-inch pegboard panel (S) on the right-hand side of the sewing machine compartment is mounted with 1 1/4-inch wood screws and special fiber spacers, which are sold wherever pegboard hardware is available. Optionally, pegboard panels may be mounted on both sides and on the rear of this compartment for greatest hang-up storage.

After puttying where necessary and sanding all surfaces (particularly the front edges of the plywood shelves and panels), a coat of primer is applied to the entire closet. An appealing finish can be achieved with contrasting dark and light enamel, or flat colors can be applied. The rear wall may be painted to match the darker door frame.

HIDE A SEWING STORAGE WALL

Now you see it, now you don't. When you see it, there are two sewing storage closets on either side of a window seat alcove (Fig. 6-5). Pull down the striped window shades, and the closets disappear. Once the portable sewing machine is removed and the hinged table (U,V,W of Fig. 6-6) swings up behind the drapes, all you see is a pleasant window seat alcove with bright yellow cushions. This sewing storage wall can be built around any window.

Refer to Table 6-3. The uprights or partitions (A) are 3/4-inch quarter-round moldings (BB,PP). The shelves (B,D) are adjustable, but you may prefer to have them fixed by nailing them through the sides of the uprights. Note that the shelves do not come out to the front edges of the uprights to permit the striped window shades to pass in front of them. On the right side, where the closets have no shelves from the middle down, there are vertical quarter-rounds (KK) behind the front strips (X,Y) to prevent the shades from swinging back into the closet.

The window seats have 2- × -2 frames (F, G,H,I,J,K) nailed to the floor, rear wall, and

Fig. 6-5. A Sewing Storage Wall.

uprights. These seats provide additional storage area and have removable covers (P,O) with finger holes. A pegboard (LL) is attached to the left side of the alcove where it is fastened with screws to the upright (A). A cleat (OO) is screwed to the bottom end of the pegboard. The top end of the sewing table (U,V,W) rests on this cleat when it swings down.

The drawer guides (II,JJ) for the four drawers at the lower left are unusually wide because of the width of the flat molding strips (X,Y). These guides can be secured to the uprights with glue and long screws.

The fascia board (E) at the top, which conceals the rollers of the shades, is wrapped in fabric stapled on the back. This piece should be fastened with finishing nails driven through the front strips (X,Y) and the forward edges of the uprights (A).

BUILD THIS HANDY ALCOVE FOR CHILDREN'S BASEMENT PLAYROOM

Here's an alcove that is constructed for a wall in a children's playroom, provides loads of extra storage space and comfortable seating, and is easy to build. In Fig. 6-7 it is shown in a converted cellar, as seen by the low ceiling. It is spaced slightly away from and independent of the walls and is attached only to the ceiling joists and floor to prevent moisture problems. It can, however, be constructed in practically any room in your house and attached to the studs in a regular plasterboard wall.

Refer to Fig. 6-8 and Table 6-4. The alcove unit consists of a shelving storage area to the right, a

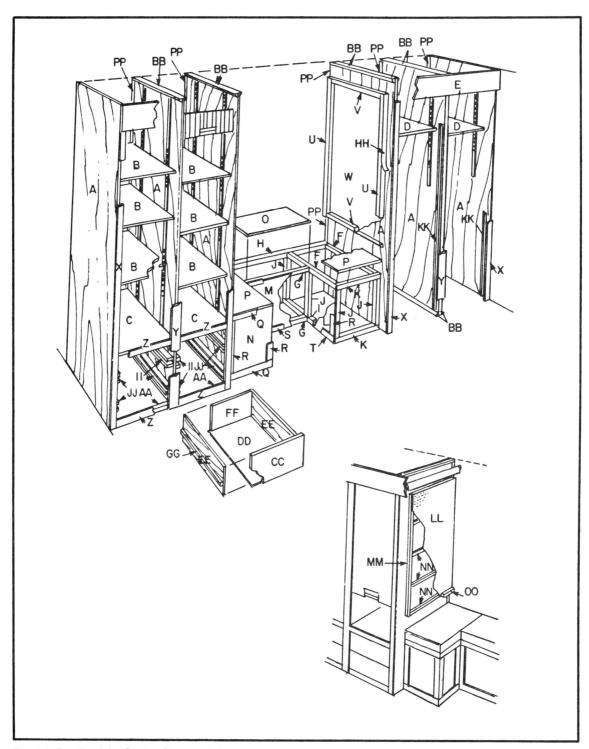

Fig. 6-6. Details of the Sewing Storage Wall.

126

Table 6-3. Materials for the Sewing Storage Wall.

A.	6 pcs, 3/4″ × 32″ × 96″	V.	2 pcs, 1 1/2″ × 1 1/2″ × 27″
B.	6 pcs, 3/4″ × 19 3/8″ × 30 1/2″	W.	1 pc,. 3/4″ × 30″ × 58 1/2″
C.	2 pcs, 3/4″ × 19 7/8″ × 32″	X.	4 pcs, 3/8″ × 2″ × 86 3/4″
D.	2 pcs, 3/4″ × 19 3/8″ × 29″	Y.	2 pcs, 3/8″ × 2 1/2″ × 86 3/4″
E.	1 pc, 1/2″ × 9 1/4″ × 144″	Z.	4 pcs, 3/8″ × 1 1/2″ × 17 1/2″
F.	4 pcs, 1 1/2″ × 1 1/2″ × 27″	AA.	2 pcs, 1 1/2″ × 1 1/2″ × 19 7/8″
G.	2 pcs, 1 1/2″ × 1 1/2″ × 24″	BB.	10 pcs, 3/4 round × 32″
H.	1 pc, 1 1/2″ × 1 1/2″ × 60″	CC.	4 pcs, 3/4″ × 5 5/8″ × 17 1/2″
I.	2 pcs, 1 1/2″ × 1 1/2″ × 28 1/2″	DD.	4 pcs, 1/4″ × 16″ × 24 1/4″
J.	8 pcs, 1 1/2″ × 1 1/2″ × 12″	EE.	8 pcs, 1/2″ × 5″ × 24″
K.	4 pcs, 1 1/2″ × 1 1/2″ × 18″	FF.	4 pcs, 1/2″ × 5″ × 15″
L.	2 pcs, 3/8″ × 15″ × 16″	GG.	8 pcs, 3/4″ × 3/4″ × 24″
M.	1 pc, 3/8″ × 15″ × 24″	HH.	1 pc, 2 1/4″ × 58 1/2″ veneer tape
N.	2 pcs, 3/8″ × 15″ × 18″	II.	8 pcs, 3/4″ × 1 1/2″ × 31″
O.	1 pc, 3/8″ × 14″ × 24″	JJ.	8 pcs, 3/4″ × 2″ × 31″
P.	2 pcs, 3/8″ × 18″ × 30″	KK.	4 pcs, 1/4-round 3/4″ × 85″
Q.	4 pcs, 1/4″ × 2″ × 18″	LL.	pegboard 30″ × 60″
R.	10 pcs, 1/4″ × 2″ × 11 3/8″	MM.	2 pcs, 3/4″ × 3/4″ × 60″
S.	4 pcs, 1/4″ × 2″ × 24″	NN.	5 pcs, 3/4″ × 3/4″ × 28 1/2″
T.	4 pcs, 1/4″ × 2″ × 16″	OO.	1 pc, 3/4″ × 3/4″ × 30″
U.	2 pcs, 1 1/2″ × 1 1/2″ × 58 1/2″	PP.	10 pcs, 1/4-round 3/4″ × 94 1/2″

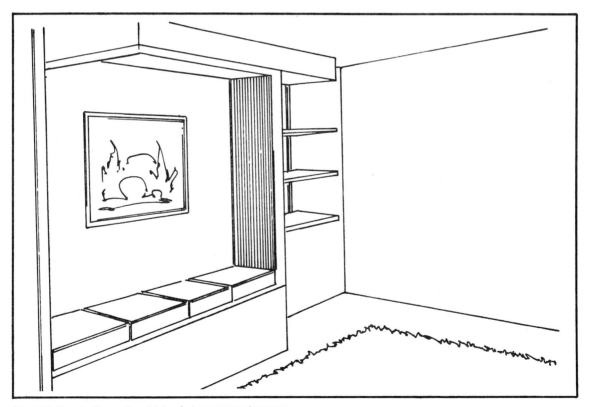

Fig. 6-7. Handy Alcove for children's basement playroom.

frame with paneling on the outsides of a recessed rectangular alcove, with a plasterboard back in the center and cushions on the alcove for seating. The area underneath the alcove was left unused in the original design, but can be easily converted to three sections of the storage area. They are accessible through paneled front doors (A) with a 1/2-inch plywood backing (B) that swing downward and are held in place by piano hinges (FF) at the bottoms. They open by touch latches (CC) rather than outside handles.

The building of the frame is simplicity itself.

It consists of rectangular box framing at the top and bottom. The top part of the frame continues on past the two vertical sides of the alcove in both directions. The top and bottom parts of the frame are nailed to the existing joists in the ceiling and floor through pieces BB and L. The framing in the top is made of 2 × 2s; in the bottom horizontal and vertical support pieces for the top are pieces W and Z; for the bottom they are pieces K and P. The sides of the alcove (J) are nailed to the top and bottom framing, and the front opening of the alcove is all covered with molding (GG, HH, II, KK, QQ, RR).

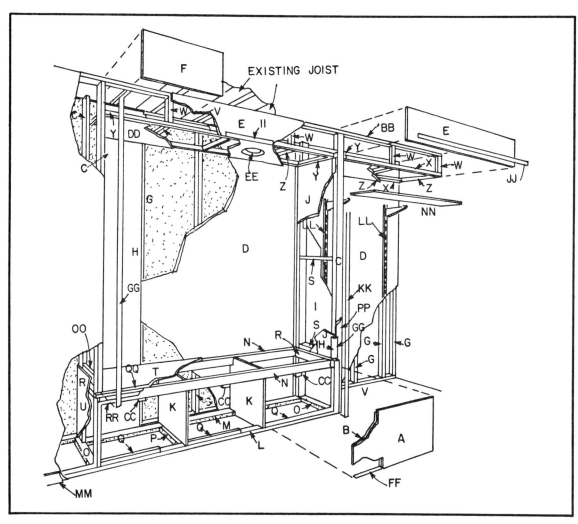

Fig. 6-8. Details of the Handy Alcove.

Table 6-4. Materials for the Handy Alcove.

A.	3 pcs, 1/4″ × 11 1/2″ × 24 1/2″ paneling		U.	1 pc, 5/8″ × 16″ × 18″ plasterboard
B.	3 pcs, 1/2″ × 9 1/2″ × 22 1/2″		V.	2 pcs, 1 1/2″ × 2 1/2″ × 144″
C.	4 pcs, 1 1/2″ × 3 1/2″ × 81″		W.	5 pcs, 1 1/2″ × 1 1/2″ × 10″
D.	2 pcs, 5/8″ × 48″ × 84″ plasterboard		X.	2 pcs, 1 1/2″ × 1 1/2″ × 41 1/2″
E.	2 pcs, 1/4″ × 13 5/8″ × 48″ paneling		Y.	3 pcs, 1 1/2″ × 1 1/2″ × 16″
F.	1 pc, 1/4″ × 13 5/8″ × 19″ paneling		Z.	3 pcs, 1 1/2″ × 1 1/2″ × 13″
			AA.	1 pc, 5/8″ × 16″ × 43″
G.	12 pcs, 1 1/2″ × 2 1/2″ × 81 1/4″		BB.	1 pc, 1 1/2″ × 1 1/2″ × 115″
H.	1 pc, 5/8″ × 20″ × 84″ plasterboard		CC.	3 touch latches
			DD.	1 pc, 5/8″ × 16″ × 68″
I.	1 pc, 5/8″ × 16″ × 71″ plasterboard		EE.	2 recessed lights
			FF.	3 piano hinges
J.	2 pcs, 5/8″ × 16″ × 55″ plasterboard		GG.	2 pcs, 1 1/2″ × 56 1/2″ molding
K.	2 pcs, 3/4″ × 16″ × 16″		HH.	2 pcs, 1 1/2″ × 55″ molding
L.	1 pc, 1 1/2″ × 3 1/2″ × 73″		II.	1 pc, 1 1/2″ × 71″ molding
M.	1 pc, 1 1/2″ × 3 1/2″ × 68″		JJ.	1 pc, 1 1/2″ × 44 1/2″ molding
N.	2 pcs, 1 1/2″ × 3 1/2″ × 65″		KK.	1 pc, 1 1/2″ × 72 1/2″ molding
O.	2 pcs, 1 1/2″ × 3 1/2″ × 12 1/2″		LL.	shelf hardware
P.	2 pcs, 1 1/2″ × 1 1/2″ × 9″		MM.	baseboard molding
Q.	3 pcs, 1 1/2″ × 1 1/2″ × 22 1/8″		NN.	3 pcs, 3/4″ × 9 1/2″ × 43″
R.	2 pcs, 1 1/2″ × 3 1/2″ × 16″		OO.	2 pcs, 1 1/2″ × 3 1/2″ × 9″
S.	4 pcs, 1 1/2″ × 3 1/2″ × 13″		PP.	1 pc, 1/4″ × 4″ × 71″
T.	1 pc, 3/4″ × 16″ × 68″		QQ.	1 pc, 3/4″ × 3/4″ × 74″ molding
			RR.	1 pc, 1 1/2″ × 71″ molding

The top part of the frame, as well as the left side of the unit and the bottom doors (B), is covered with paneling (E,F,A).

The recessed plasterboard (D) in both the alcove and the shelving area to the right are supported by 2 × 4s (G) nailed to the top and bottom of the framing—three for the center piece and two for the shelving area. The two center supports for the shelving area are particularly important because they support the standards (LL) for the shelves (NN). Having standards for the shelving instead of individual brackets fastened to the supports allows you to change the shelving arrangement at any time according to your needs. The plans also include a recessed light (EE) in the alcove soffit above the seating cushions.

Chapter 7

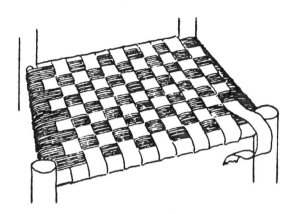

Shaker Furniture

Shaker furniture is easy to make and incredibly useful. The projects in this chapter will add beauty and charm to your home, and everyone will be sure to marvel at the Shaker reproductions you have made.

MAKE A SHAKER BENCH

Here's a delightful bench that has all the charm, grace, and simplicity of Shaker craftmanship (Fig. 7-1). It's very easy to build because it consists of only seven parts. You can make this bench from the parts described in Table 7-1 and shown in Fig. 7-2.

The first step in the assembly of the parts is to place the seat top (C) face down on the floor (Fig. 7-3). Then place the seat support (D) in the center of the underside of the seat, which is now facing upward. The slots and predrilled screw holes of the seat support (D) should face upward and should be directly over the dado or groove in the underside of the seat that crosses its width.

To make sure that the seat support (D) is prop-

erly in position, place the slot in one of the legs (E) over the slot in the seat support so that both slots interlock (Fig. 7-4). Then press the leg down firmly into its own dado. Using a hammer and block of wood, tap the edge of the leg so that it lines up flush with the edge of the seat, as shown in Fig. 7-5. For good measure, also tap the leg down into its groove with the block and hammer. Repeat this operation with the remaining leg at the other end of the seat support. All this should be done without glue or screws.

You now have the seat support in precisely the right position. Mark this position accurately with a pencil and remove both the seat support (D) and the legs (E). Apply glue to the top of the seat support, place it in the marked position, and drive screws through the predrilled holes into the underside of the seat (Figs. 7-6 and 7-7).

Glue should then be applied to the slot and upper edges of the legs. With a hammer and block of wood, drive the legs down firmly so that their slots interlock with those of the seat support, and their upper edges are seated in the dadoes that

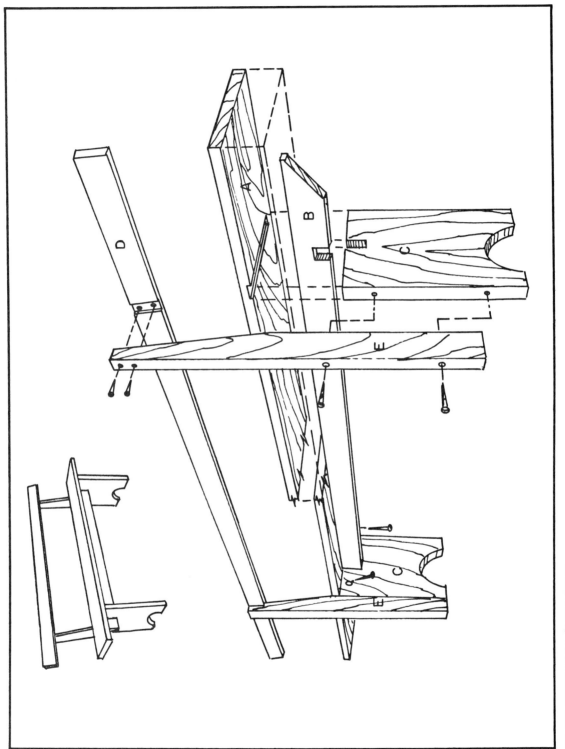

Fig. 7-1. Details of the Shaker Bench.

A.	1 pc, 60" × 3" × 3/4"
B.	2 pcs, 29 7/8" × 3" × 1 1/4"
C.	1 pc, 60" × 9 3/4" × 1 1/4"
D.	1 pc, 54" × 4" × 3/4"
E.	2 pcs, 16" × 9 3/4" × 1 1/4"

Table 7-1. Materials for the Shaker Bench.

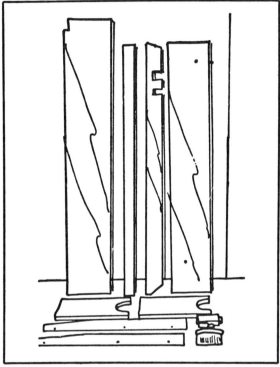

Fig. 7-2. The seven basic structural parts of the Shaker Bench are shown.

Fig. 7-3. Assembly begins by properly lining up the seat support and seat top.

Fig. 7-4. Seat legs and now set into place. Note that slots in the leg and support interlock and that the leg top fits into the dado which has been precut on the underside of the seat top.

Fig. 7-5. A hammer and block of wood are used to ensure a flush line along the back of the leg and seat top. Then positioning is marked with a pencil, and the legs and support are removed so that glue can be applied.

Fig. 7-6. The support and legs are finally fastened, using the proper length of roundhead screws.

Fig. 7-7. The simplicity of the bench assembly is evident in this illustration, which shows the final fastening of the leg support pieces to the bench top. A glue and screwdriver are the only required tools.

Fig. 7-8. With the bench placed on its front edge, the back rest supports are positioned. Glue has already been applied.

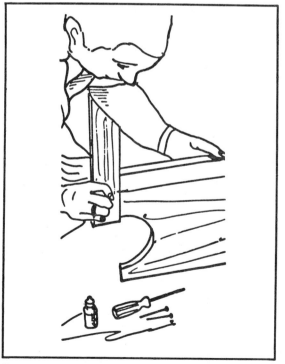

Fig. 7-9. Flush line-up with the leg bottoms is important. Again a wooden block is used as a straightedge.

cross the width of the seat. The legs should also be fastened with the 2-inch screws.

Place the assembly with its front edges face down on the floor (Figs. 7-8 and 7-9). Now attach the supports (B) for the back rest with glue and 2 1/2-inch screws, driving the screws through the predrilled holes into the back edges of the legs (E) (Fig. 7-10). Make sure that the bottoms of the back rest supports are flush with those of the legs.

Now put the assembly on its legs. Using glue and 1-inch screws, attach the back rest (A) to its supports. These supports (B) should be inserted into the grooves at the back of the back rest. The tops of the supports should be flush with the top of the back rest. Glue and tap the hole buttons into the holes in the back supports (B), tapered ends first (Fig. 7-11).

Remove excess glue from all joints with a dry rag and allow the glue to dry overnight. Lightly

Fig. 7-10. The 2 1/2-inch screws are driven home through the back supports and into the bench legs. Note how all of the joints are square and even.

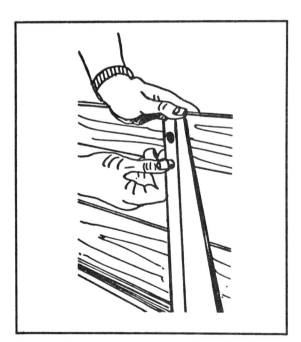

Fig. 7-11. The back rest has been joined to the supports, and hole buttons are being inserted to finish the assembly. After you wipe the glued joints and allow the glue to dry overnight, you can sand, stain, and finish the bench using shellac, varnish, and paste wax.

sand the bench with sandpaper 100-grit. Finish with medium walnut stain. After the stain has dried overnight, apply white shellac thinned half and half with alcohol, and rub with fine steel wool when it is dry. Follow with two coats of light varnish, sanding each coat when dry. Finish with paste wax buffed to a satin glow.

BUILD THIS SHAKER ARMCHAIR

Shaker furniture has become so popular with American home owners that kits have become available which make it possible for persons without any special woodworking skill to assemble an authentic piece which cannot be distinguished from the real thing. In one such kit of a ladderback arm chair, all the parts are supplied with predrilled holes or slots for arms and rails (Fig. 7-12). The back with

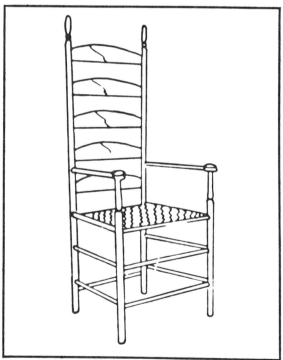

Fig. 7-12. The Shaker Armchair.

its six curved slats is preassembled in this kit. You can also make a chair from scratch. Assembly is very easy.

Chair Assembly

The entire chair is assembled loosely without glue to see if all the parts fit. It may be necessary to sand the ends of rails slightly if too tight a fit has resulted from absorption of moisture during shipment. The chair is then disassembled, and the position of each part noted.

When you are ready for final assembly, apply glue with a small stick to the walls of the holes into which the rails fit (Fig. 7-13). Do not apply glue to the ends of the rails because they may swell rapidly and make it very difficult to assemble the chair.

Glue and assemble the two front corner posts and three long rails, making sure that the rail with the largest diameter goes on top (Fig. 7-14). (The rails of the seat all have a larger diameter than the others.) Note that the front rails go into the holes on the front posts that are slightly lower than the side rail holes. To ensure tight joints, place the assembly on its side and pound with a hammer and small block of wood (Fig. 7-15). Now lay the

assembly on a flat and make sure the legs are parallel. If they are not, twist the assembly until they are.

The side rails are then glued and assembled to the front post and the preassembled back after the arms have been placed over the front posts and secured with post caps (Figs. 7-16 through 7-18).

With front legs lying on the floor, pound the back legs with a hammer and block of wood to ensure a tight fit (Fig. 7-19). Using a dry rag, remove all excess glue from the joints (Fig. 7-20).

The chair should be checked for alignment before the glue dries. All four legs should rest squarely on a level surface. If they do not, bounce the chair frame lightly on the leg that appears too long until all four legs rest on the floor.

Measure the diagonal distance between the front and back posts. If they are not equal, put a rope around the longest diagonal and tighten by inserting a stick between the ropes and twisting until the distances are equal. Do not remove the rope until the glue dries, which should be in about 24 hours.

The chair should then be lightly sanded with sandpaper. Stain for the finish is in a can that comes

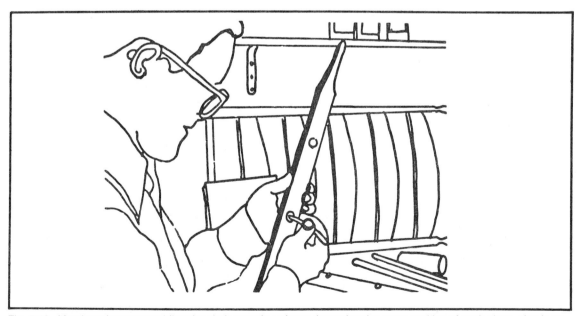

Fig. 7-13. After loosely preassembling the chair parts in order to determine the exact position of each piece, glue is applied to the front post holes.

Fig. 7-14. Long rails are inserted into the front corner posts, making sure that the rails with the largest diameters go at the top to receive the seat taping.

Fig. 7-15. Joints in the chair front assembly are secured by tapping the posts from the side, using a hammer and wood block to prevent damaging the leg.

138

Fig. 7-16. Six remaining side rails are inserted into their respective holes in the front posts after alignment has been checked and glue is applied.

Fig. 7-17. Chair arms are mounted onto front posts after you dab a small amount of glue inside the arm hole. Any excess glue is wiped off.

Fig. 7-18. Front and side rail assembly is joined to the preassembled back by inserting the side rails into their respective holes after you apply the glue.

Fig. 7-19. Glued joints are then tightened, again using a hammer and wooden block, and front post caps are glued to the two protruding tenons.

Fig. 7-20. Wiping off excess glue around all joints is an important step. If left on the surface, glue would prevent the stain from penetrating the wood.

with the kit (Fig. 7-21). Suggestions for finishing are on the stain can.

After staining, two coats of clear varnish may be applied, each of which should be rubbed with very fine steel wool (Fig. 7-22). An oil finish is available from the manufacturer of the kit. Liquid furniture polish or paste wax can be applied for greater luster and added protection.

For those who wish to make this armchair from scratch and have a lathe to make all the turnings, the dimensions are available in Table 7-2 and Fig. 7-23. Be sure to use a good grade of birch or maple. The curved slats of the back may present something of a problem since they are usually shaped or bent by steaming and pressure in a special press. You can, however, cut them out of a solid block of birch if you have access to a bandsaw and thus secure the curved shape. Otherwise your only alternative is to make these back slats flat.

Weaving the Seat

One of the most distinctive features of Shaker chairs are seats woven of tape which the Shakers called *listing*. This cloth tape, in two different colors is supplied in the kit. Of course, rush, splint, and cane seats were also used by the Shakers, but the woven tape seats were the most popular.

The first step in seating the chair is known as *warping*. This process simply entails wrapping tape around the front and back rails to provide a warp both on the top and the bottom of the seat (Fig. 7-24). The procedure is as follows: the end (doubled over for strength) of one coil of tape is tacked to the inner side of the back rail as close as possible to the left back post; this doubled-over end must point toward the top of the chair (Fig. 7-25). With the end firmly tacked in place, the coil of tape is brought over the back rail to the front rail at right angles to both the front and back rails. It is then brought over the front rail and returned to the back rail, which it goes under and over. It is essential that the tape not be twisted.

This procedure is continued until the back right post is reached, and there is no space for another warp on the back rail (there will, however, be spaces at either side on the front rail). When this

Fig. 7-21. After a preliminary touch-up sanding, the stain is wiped on with a rag. Brush application would be slower, but would make less mess.

Fig. 7-22. The stain is allowed to dry overnight and then clear varnish is applied in one or more coats, with careful rubbing with steel wool between coats.

142

Table 7-2. Materials for the Shaker Armchair.

A.	5 pcs, 17 5/8" × 3 1/4" × 9/32"
B.	2 pcs, 1 1/4" × 47"
C.	2 pcs, 1 1/4" × 4 1/2"
D.	4 pcs, dowel 1/2" × 1 1/2"
E.	10 pcs, dowel 1/4" × 1"
F.	2 pcs, 17" × 3" × 5/8"
G.	2 pcs, 5/8" × 2"
H.	2 pcs, 27" × 1 3/8"
I.	4 pcs, 16 3/4" × 3/4"
J.	1 pc, 17 5/8" × 3/4"
K.	1 pc, 21 7/8" × 7/8"
L.	2 pcs, 21 7/8" × 3/4"
II.	2 pcs, 16 3/4" × 7/8"
JJ.	1 pc, 17 5/8" × 7/8"

stage is reached, the tape is brought over and under the front rail to the back rail and cut off, allowing about 2 extra inches. This end is doubled over and securely tacked to the bottom right side of the back rail, where it will overlap the last warp strip. Before this end is tacked in place, it is important that as much slack in the warping as possible be pulled out; the tape should not be stretched, but it should be firm. It should be emphasized that the tape must run at right angles to the front and back rails. Because the side rails are splayed from front to back, there will be a triangular-shaped area on either side of the seat which will be without warps. These warps will be added at a later stage.

With the warping completed, the next step is the actual weaving of the seat. Begin by securing the end of the coil of tape, which will be the *weft*. The end (doubled over for strength) is tacked to the inside of the left side rail as close as possible to the left back post (Fig. 7-26). The pad, which has been made to fill the area of the seat, is now stuffed between the top and bottom levels of the warping (Fig. 7-27). The free end of the coil of tape is then brought over the first warp strip of the top layer, under the next, over one, under one, etc., until the right back post is reached. The full length of the tape is now pulled through all the top layer of warp strips (Fig. 7-28). The chair is then turned over, and

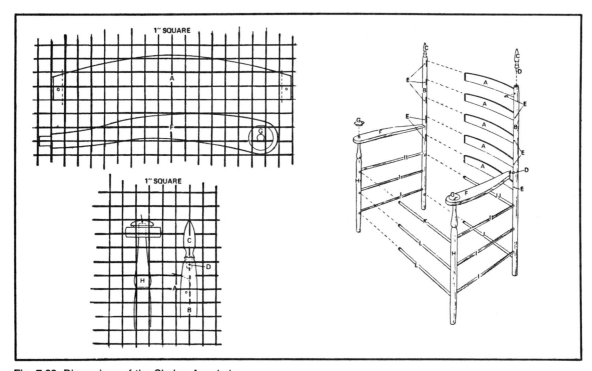

Fig. 7-23. Dimensions of the Shaker Armchair.

Fig. 7-24. The first step in weaving the chair seat is wrapping tape from the front to the back rungs, after first tacking it inside the back rail.

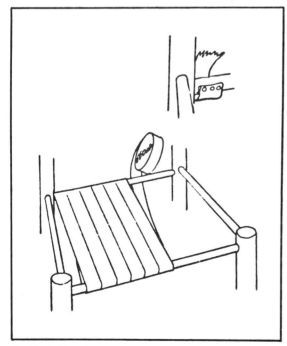

Fig. 7-25. The double-over end must point toward the top of the chair. The tape is wrapped under the back rung and over the front rung.

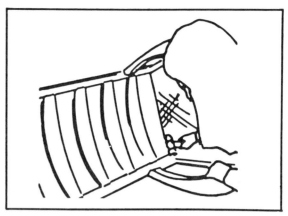

Fig. 7-26. The cross weaving, or weft, tape is now tacked to the bottom portion of the rear left seat rung, and the wefting is begun.

Fig. 7-27. When the warp is tightened and tacked, the cut foam pad is inserted between the rows or warping.

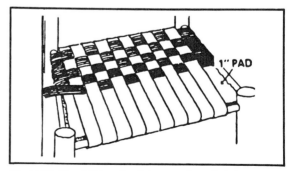

Fig. 7-28. The full length of the tape is pulled through all the top layer of warp strips.

144

the process is repeated on the lower layer of warp strips.

Next, the weft is again woven through the top layer of warp strips, this time starting under the first strip, over the second, etc., so that the result is the start of a checkerboard pattern. The chair is again turned over, and the weft is returned through the lower level of warp strips so as to form, as on the top layer, the beginning of a checkerboard pattern. It will be noted that, at the right side of the chair, the end warp of the bottom layer (which has been tacked to the right side of the back rail) will somewhat overlap the second to the last warp on the same side. It is essential that these two be treated as a single warp, i.e., the weft must be carried over or under both of them together. Only in this way can a checkerboard pattern be created on the bottom of the seat; in the finished seat, this inconsistency will not be apparent.

Keeping Weft Flat

The process just described is continued until the weft reaches the front posts of the chair. Again, it must be emphasized that the tape must not be twisted (Fig. 7-29). Also, it should be pulled firmly each time it is brought through the warp strips, and

Fig. 7-29. Remember that the tape should not be twisted. Doing so would create a visible lump in the finished flat seat.

the rows should be kept as straight as possible, each touching the last. The final row on the top of the seat will abut the front posts on the side rails and should curve slightly toward the front rail to keep the warps smooth and flat. Because at this stage the warps will be tight, a dinner knife is useful for lifting them to permit the weft to pass under them (Fig. 7-30). The weft is now cut so that it will end on the bottom of the chair and is tacked to the left side rail as close as possible to the left front post. If there is not sufficient room to weave it through to the left side of the chair, as is sometimes the case, it should be tacked to the bottom of the front rail (Fig. 7-31).

Splicing the Weft

If it is necessary to splice the weft, it should be done so that the splice falls on the bottom of the seat. In splicing, the ends of the tape should be firmly sewed together.

The final step in taping the chair is that of filling in the corners of the seat with added warps (Fig. 7-32). For this, two strips of tape of the color used in the warping are cut to a length which will allow them to run from the front rail to the back on both the top and the bottom of the seat (i.e., double the depth of the chair) with 2 or 3 inches to spare. They are then woven in parallel to the last warp on either side of the top of the seat, are brought over the front rail, and are similarly woven on the bot-

Fig. 7-30. When the weaving is complete, the chair seat should resemble this illustration.

145

Fig. 7-31. A view of the underside of the chair while the weft is being completed. The tightened weft will be tacked to the left front rung bottom.

tom. The ends, meeting at the back rail, are then tacked in place as inconspicuously as possible on the bottom of the back rail.

One (or sometimes two or three, depending on the size and type of the chair) additional warp will be required on either side of the seat to fill out the warping near the front posts. Because of the triangular shape of the areas to be filled in, these warps cannot be carried back to the back posts of the chair, but should be woven through the wefts until they meet the side rails. Their ends should be tucked under the wefts and secured either by tacking to the side rails (tacking them under a weft, which may be lifted with a dinner knife) or by carefully gluing them to the bottom of the weft with cloth glue.

Putting in these added warps demands care. The quality of the finished seat depends to a great extent on the workmanship of this finishing stage. If done with care, the seat will fill out smoothly at the front.

CONSTRUCT A SHAKER DROP-LEAF TABLE

If you are a lover of Shaker furniture, you will find this large drop-leaf table a very attractive project

(Fig. 7-33). Based on a Shaker original made about 1830 at the Hancock, Mass., Shaker community, this table with its long rectangular top and broad side leaves takes up little space when closed, yet opens up to a width of 38 inches when the leaves are raised.

You can make this table by cutting all the pieces as shown in Fig. 7-34 and Table 7-3, or you can make the whole table from a kit with precision-cut parts (Fig. 7-35). The kit is supplied by Shaker Workshops, Inc., Box 710, Concord, Mass. 01742.

Assemble the legs and skirts first. Select a right leg and a left leg and place them so that they face each other. Apply glue to the slots (mortises) in each leg. Do not apply glue to the tenons (tongues) of the skirts because they may swell rapidly and make it impossible to get them into the mortises. Line up the holes bored through mortise-and-tenon joints, then glue and insert the 1/4-inch pegs (Fig. 7-36). Start with one of the short skirts. Repeat this procedure with the remaining short skirt and the other two legs. Then add the long skirts to the remaining mortises in the legs already glued to the short skirts, pinning them with pegs as just described (Fig. 7-37).

Fig. 7-32. Corner filling with shorter pieces of tape is the final step in the seat work. Tacks or glue will anchor the tape ends.

Fig. 7-33. The completed Shaker Drop-Leaf Table.

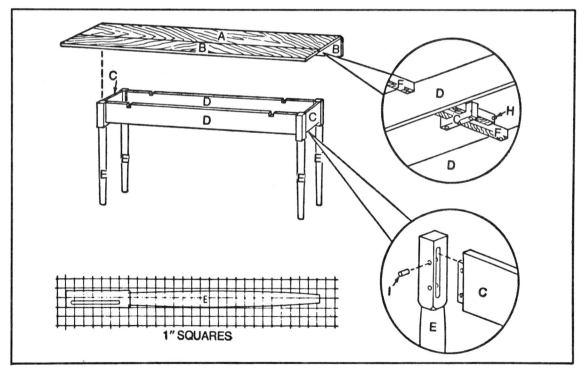

1" SQUARES

Fig. 7-34. Dimensions of the Shaker Drop-Leaf Table.

147

Table 7-3. Materials for the Shaker Drop-Leaf Table.

A.	1 pc, 19" × 72" × 3/4"
B.	2 pcs, 10 1/8" × 73" × 3/4"
C.	2 pcs, 6 1/8" × 14 1/4" × 3/4"
D.	2 pcs, 6 1/8" × 57 1/2" × 3/4"
E.	4 pcs, 1 3/4" dia. × 28 1/4"
F.	4 pcs, 1 1/4" × 16 1/2" × 1"
G.	2 pcs, 2" × 5 1/2" × 1"
H.	4 pcs, 3/8" dia. × 1 1/4"
I.	16 pcs, 1/4" dia. × 1 3/8"
J.	6 pcs, #10 × 2" screws
K.	10 pcs, #10 × 1 1/4" screws
L.	36 pcs, #8 × 1/2" screws

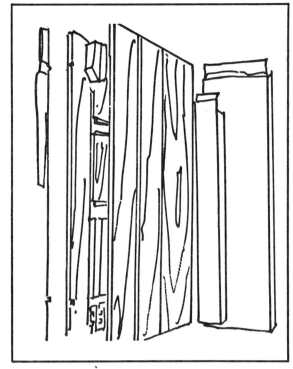

Note that all of the skirts have screw holes bored at a slant through the upper edges. These edges will be in contact with the underside of the table top. When assembling the skirts and legs, it is very important that all these skirt edges with holes face upward (Fig. 7-38). Also be sure that all these screw hole space inward. Remove all excess glue at once with a dry cloth.

Because of the size of this table, it is suggested that the legs and skirt assembly, drop leaves, top,

Fig. 7-35. Pieces of the Shaker Drop-Leaf Table.

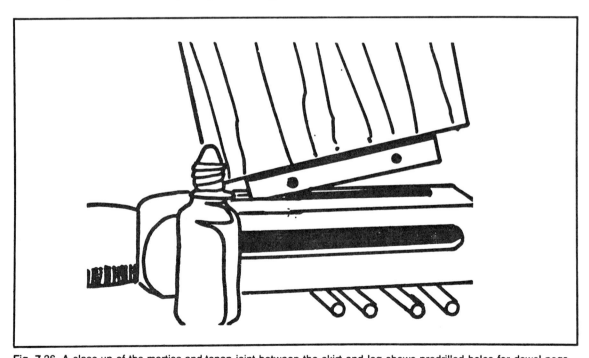

Fig. 7-36. A close-up of the mortise-and-tenon joint between the skirt and leg shows predrilled holes for dowel pegs.

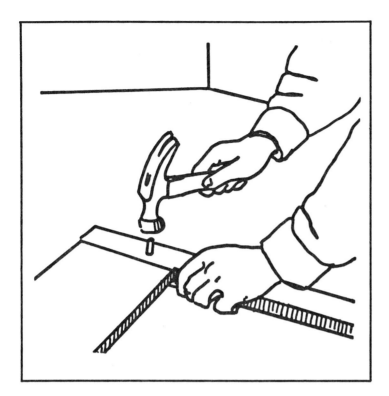

Fig. 7-37. The peg is being driven into the table end assembly. A work mat protects the carpeted floor from sawdust and glue staining.

Fig. 7-38. Here the side skirts are being jointed to the end assembly. Make sure the slide cutouts and screw holes in the skirt are facing the tops of the legs.

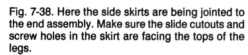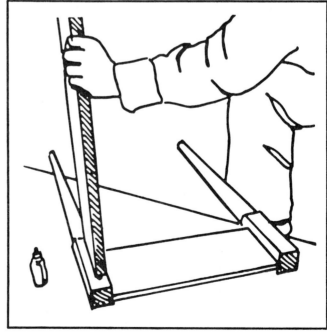

Fig. 7-39. The table should be stained and finished before the top and leaves are joined to the base to make the job easier.

and support slides be stained and finished before complete assembly (Fig. 7-39).

Attach the leaves to the table top using three hinges for each leaf. The holes in the hinges should line up with the predrilled pilot holes in the undersides of the leaves and the table top (Fig. 7-40). Use the 1/2-inch screws in the kit and be sure to attach the long side of each hinge to the leaves.

Fig. 7-40. Begin the final assembly by attaching the leaves to the top. Hinges and 1/2-inch screws are aligned to predrilled holes.

Place the assembled table top and leaves face down on the floor. Now place the legs and skirt assembly exactly in the center of the underside of the table now facing up toward you.

With a pencil or nail inserted in the holes of the skirts, mark the underside of the table for pilot screw holes (Fig. 7-41). Using a 1/8-inch drill bit, drill holes not more than 1/2-inch deep at the same

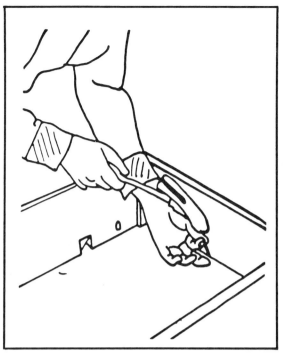

Fig. 7-41. With the base assembly centered over the open top, a nail or center punch is used to locate pilot holes for joining the two table pieces.

Fig. 7-43. The base and top assemblies are again recentered and fastened using 1 1/2-inch roundhead screws. Note the angled, precountersunk holes in the skirt.

Fig. 7-42. The base assembly is slid aside for pilot-hole drilling at a 30-degree angle. Masking tape wrapped around the drill bit acts as a visual stop.

Fig. 7-44. The slides and slide guides are held in position while the pilot holes are marked carefully, as in Fig. 7-41.

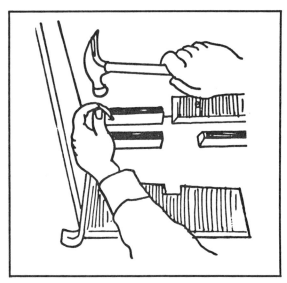

Fig. 7-45. When the slide guides are fastened, the slide-stop dowels are driven into place. They will keep the slides from pulling out completely.

Fig. 7-46. The finishing of the top and leaves is the final step in the table assembly. Here a final coat of the satin varnish is being applied.

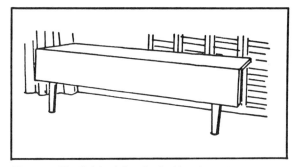

Fig. 7-47. The finished drop-leaf table, shown folded down.

angle as those in the skirts (Fig. 7-42). Do not drive screws without pilot holes into the bottom of the table top or you may split it. To achieve the proper angle, get a 1/8-inch drill bit, which is longer than usual for this size, and use the holes in the skirts as guides. The skirts should be fastened with ten 1 1/4-inch screws (Fig. 7-43).

The final job is the installation of the support slides, which hold up the hinged leaves and their guides. There are two support slides under each leaf. Insert these slides in the holes in the skirts. The guides for these support slides have three holes in them and notches that fit the slides. The guides are placed equidistant from the long skirts with their notches or dadoes over the slides. Mark spots on the underside of the table through the holes in the guides (Fig. 7-44). Drill pilot holes at these spots that are no deeper than 1/2 inch. Attach the two slide guides with 2-inch screws. Now glue and insert the 3/8-inch slide stopper dowels in the holes in the sides of the slide bars. Make certain that these stop dowels face away from each other, as shown in Fig. 7-45.

Finish with alcohol and water-resistant varnish, using two coats on the table top and leaves (Fig. 7-46). An oil finish of boiled linseed oil and turpentine in equal parts can also be used. Finally, use a good grade of paste wax to protect the finish and buff to a soft glow. The finished project is shown in Fig. 7-47.

Chapter 8

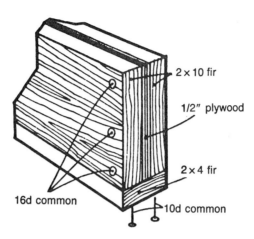

2 x 10 fir

1/2" plywood

2 x 4 fir

16d common

10d common

Home-Improvement Projects

For a change of pace, try any or all of the projects in this chapter. You'll find out how you can use wood beams to add unusual beauty to your home, how to refinish wood floors, how to use cedar shingles, even how to build and panel a closet! All will add uniqueness and attractiveness to your home, and all are worth the time spent on them.

DRAMATIZE WITH WOOD BEAMS

Do-it-yourselfers can give almost any room in their house a rustic, Old English, or Spanish look in a few hours with realistic, wood-grained, vinyl-covered hardboard ceiling beams at a fraction of the cost and weight of wood beams. Hardboard beams won't swell or crack, but will give long maintenance-free service. These beams can also be used on walls or to hide joints when you are installing new wallboard.

Before installing the beams, make a scale drawing of the arrangement you like, parallel or crisscrossed, which will also tell you how much to get. Let the beams set in the room where you're going to install them for 2 days so they'll get used to the temperature/humidity conditions of the room. In this way, shrinkage or expansion will be minimized when the board are actually installed.

Essentially the beams, which come flat, are cut, glued (Fig. 8-1) and folded into a channel (Fig. 8-2) whose sides are attached by brads to furring strips already nailed to ceiling or wall joists (Fig. 8-3). For corner installations, two furring strips are used, but one side of the channel is cut off, and the bottom and other side are attached to the furring strip the same as before. For crossing patterns, simply run furring strips at right angles to one another (Fig. 8-4). Gaps should be left between the furring strips and any surface they meet, regardless of whether it's another furring strip, wall, or ceiling. To cover any joints, strip back the vinyl covering, cut the hardboard, and pull the vinyl over the joint, maintaining enough tension for a smooth fit. All brads are set below the surface and touched up with walnut-colored putty sticks. Excess putty is wiped off with a water-moistened rag.

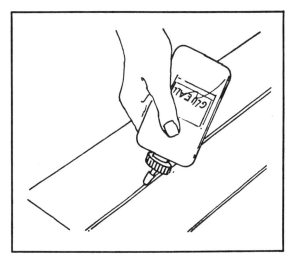

Fig. 8-1. First glue the panels.

REFINISH WOOD FLOORS

Floored by the look of your hardwood floors? Take courage. You can refinish those wooden floors that look terrible without the help of a professional with these easy step-by-step instructions. At the end of

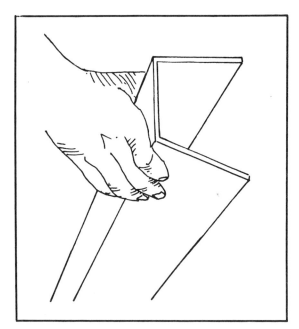

Fig. 8-2. Then fold the glued panels into channels.

Fig. 8-3. Now attach the beams to the ceiling or wall furring strips with small nails.

your refinishing project, you can have a floor with a brilliant gleam that brings out the full natural beauty of its wood. You will also lessen future floor-cleaning chores.

First, remove all the furnishings in the room. Make a thorough inspection of the floor. Fasten any boards that are loose; replace any broken or badly split boards, and countersink any protruding nail heads (Fig. 8-5). Remove the shoe molding all the

Fig. 8-4. The first step in installing these beams, is to screw or use molly bolts to attach soft wood furring strips to the ceiling joists or wall.

Fig. 8-5. Be certain to countersink any protruding nail heads before you start sanding.

way around the room, handling it very carefully to prevent its breaking (Fig. 8-6). With the shoe molding removed, you will be able to sand closer to the wall.

To prepare old hardwood floors for correct finishing, all previous finishes must be completely removed, and the surface must be bare, clean, smooth, dust-free, wax-free, and dry. Power-sanding is the most practical and effective method of removing old finishes (Fig. 8-7). You can rent the two machines necessary for the project—a drum sander and a disc edge sander—at a local paint, hardware, or tool rental store. The rental fee will be nominal, and an ample supply of sandpaper will be furnished with the machine. You will pay only for the paper you use and a minimal hourly charge for the use of the machines.

While you sand, wear clean, soft-soled shoes. The floor will have to be sanded three times. The first sanding is done to remove the old finish down to the bare wood. Using coarse sandpaper in the machine, pass the drum sander slowly over the floor lengthwise with the floor boards, starting at one wall and moving straight toward the opposite wall. Then walking backwards, pull the sander back along the same path, which enables the machine to pick up the dust created by the first pass. Each complete pass should overlap the previous pass by

Fig. 8-6. One of the first steps in refinishing your floor is to remove the shoe molding all the way around the room to enable you to sand closer to the wall. Handle the molding carefully to keep from breaking it.

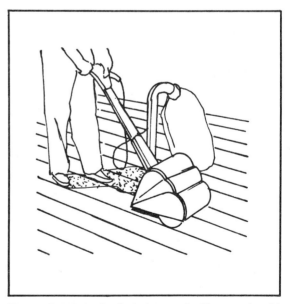

Fig. 8-7. Power sanding is the best method for removing old finish. A drum sander and disc edge sander may both be obtained from a local tool rental store.

Fig. 8-8. After sanding with the power sander, you may find areas you need to touch up by hand sanding.

2 to 3 inches. Follow this procedure throughout the entire sanding of the floor. Some refinishers do prefer diagonal sanding of the first cut. If you use this method, remember that any cross-grain sanding must be followed by lengthwise sanding with the same sandpaper.

Never stop the forward motion of the sanding machine while the sanding drum is in contact with the floor. If the machine is allowed to stay too long in one place, deep cuts or grooves in the floor will result.

The second sanding removes the roughness caused by the coarse sandpaper you used the first time over the floor. Change the coarse sandpaper to medium sandpaper and move the drum sander at a slow-to-medium rate of walking speed.

The final sanding gives you a perfectly smooth surface. Use fine sandpaper in the machine and increase your rate of walking speed considerably. When this is completed, you may wish to smooth up certain areas with sandpaper by hand (Fig. 8-8). After each of the three sandings with the drum sander, the disc sander is used (changing the sandpaper each time to correspond with what was used in the drum sander) to finish up in areas inaccessible to the drum sander, such as along baseboards and stair treads (Fig. 8-9). To remove the old finish from corners, behind radiator pipes, or in other areas inaccessible to the disc edge sander, use a hand scraper.

Dust causes more failures in floor finishing than any other single factor. Therefore, after you have completed the sanding, it is essential that you

Fig. 8-9. The disc edge sander is used in areas where the drum sander cannot reach, especially along baseboard.

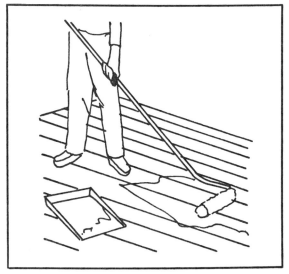

Fig. 8-10. Apply the urethane finish with a long-handled, short-napped roller. Two coats are usually enough, although you may wish to apply a third.

remove all the dust from the floor with a vacuum cleaner, dry cloth, brush, or dry mop. Vacuuming would be best to ensure a clean floor before you apply the finish.

Now you are ready to apply a urethane finish, which will give your floor a protective, hard plastic coating (Fig. 8-10). Urethane finishes have become very popular, and it is now possible to get a highly durable clear finish with these products. Application is easy: use a short napped roller with a long handle. The urethane finish is self-leveling and fast-drying. You may find it desirable to apply another coat in a few hours. If you use a urethane product, you should lightly hand sand the floor with fine sandpaper to ensure a really smooth finish before the second coat is applied. Two coats of finish are usually sufficient, although a third coat will produce a higher gloss and provide additional wear. The final coat should dry overnight.

No waxing will ever be needed. Simple dusting with a dry mop or wiping with a damp cloth will usually be enough to keep the floors clean. A urethane type finish may be repaired and renewed without the need for complete removal of the old finish. Should the finish eventually show signs of wear in heavy traffic areas, you can apply a fresh coat of finish after first cleaning the area thoroughly.

When you are satisfied with the finish, nail the shoe molding back into place, and the job is done.

USE CEDAR SHINGLES TO BEAUTIFY AN INTERIOR WALL

Red cedar shingles are ordinarily used for exterior siding, but their use for interior textured accent walls has been very successful on the West Coast. The shingles shown in Fig. 8-11 are of varying

Fig. 8-11. Cedar shingles on a wall.

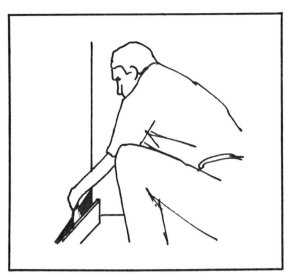

Fig. 8-12. Begin by removing the baseboard or base molding with a broad chisel and hammer.

widths and are glued to a thin plywood backer board 4 feet long. The shingles are alternately 12 1/2 and 15 1/2 inches high and taper from 1/4 inch thickness at the bottom to about 1/8 inch at the top. The backer board, which is only 3/16 inch thick, not only unites the shingles, but also makes them self-aligning since each overlapping course rests on the bottom edge of this 8-inch board.

Installation is essentially a hammer-and-nail job and is very simple. The first step is to pry away the baseboard molding at the foot of the wall with a hammer and chisel or with a thin-edged steel pry bar (Fig. 8-12).

The second step is to turn over several of the 4-foot cedar shingle strips on their backs and trim off the shingles right up to the lower edge of the backer board (Fig. 8-13). The trimming can be done with a hand or power saw. These shortened strips become starter panels with their bottoms touching the floor (Fig. 8-14).

Before you cut any panels, check the floor at the foot of the wall to see if it has sagged. An easy way to check is to turn a panel or strip upside down and place it against the wall with the straightedge resting on the floor. Do this all along the length of the wall. If any gaps show under the straightedge, the floor has sagged.

To cover these slight gaps, strike a straight line along the length of the wall about 7 inches from the floor using a carpenter's level. Then cut the bottoms of the panels with a fine tooth saw to conform with the curvature of the floor.

Another way to cover gaps between the bottoms of the cut-down panels and the floor is to use a 3/4-inch molding, either of the cove type or a quarter round. If you choose to use this method of hiding small gaps, strike a straight line the length of the

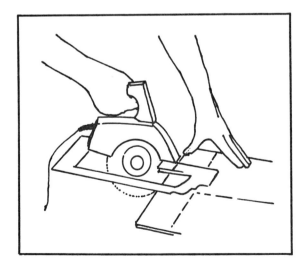

Fig. 8-13. Starting shingles are trimmed flush with the bottom edge of the backboard on the reverse side.

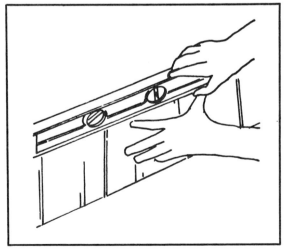

Fig. 8-14. Cut-down shingle panels are placed on the floor against the wall and are then carefully leveled.

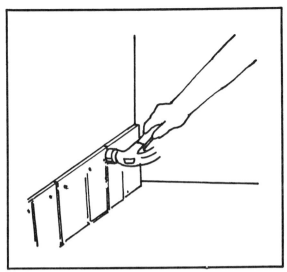

Fig. 8-15. Starter panels are nailed about 1 inch from the top. Nails are driven into wall studs.

wall with the aid of a level 8 inches up from the floor. (The cut strips are 8 inches high.) Align the tops of the shingle strips with the line you have drawn and fasten the strips with nails driven through the plasterboard and into the studs (Fig. 8-15). The molding should be fastened in the same manner with countersunk finishing nails and nail holes filled with putty. The molding should not be

nailed to the floor, or the floor will not be able to expand and contract freely.

All the pieces cut off from the strips should be saved. You will use them in completing the final course at the top of the wall.

Once the bottom strips have been nailed to the wall, the next course is mounted over them and nailed in place (Fig. 8-16). Each strip is placed so that the bottom edge of its backer board sits on top of the strip below it (Fig. 8-17). Nails are driven through each strip about an inch from the top. The nails do not show because they are covered by the strip above.

As long as you are working on plasterboard it does not matter if the end of a strip does not coincide with a stud because each strip will cover at least two studs to which it can be nailed. If, however, you are attaching the strips directly to open studs, one or more of them will have to be trimmed so that their ends can be nailed to a stud.

Openings for electrical outlets and switches can be cut with a saber saw or with hand tools such as keyhole or coping saws.

The last course at the top is made up of individual shingles left over from forming the starting course (Fig. 8-18). Use two nails for each shingle and alternate long and short pieces. At the top of

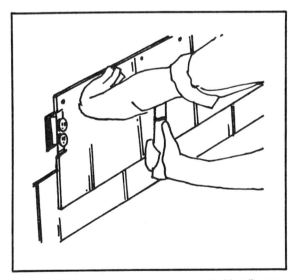

Fig. 8-16. The first course of panels is applied with nails every 16 inches, four nails per panel.

Fig. 8-17. The plywood backer board on the reverse side rests on the panel below, permitting easy application.

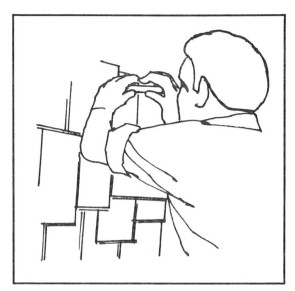

Fig. 8-18. The final course up against the ceiling is applied using individual pieces from the starter panels.

the wall, your nails will be driven into the top place—the horizontal 2 × 4 on top of the studs—so you don't have to worry about finding a stud.

The final step is fastening a molding up against the ceiling to conceal the nails used to attach the individual shingles of the top course (Fig. 8-19). The procedure is the same as for the bottom molding, if you have used one. The moldings can be stained to match the natural color of the cedar shingle strips.

So far we have talked about covering plasterboard walls. Suppose you decide to cover a concrete wall in a basement recreation room. This poses no problem. Use furring strips 1/2 inch thick and 3 inches wide and apply them horizontally to the concrete wall (Fig. 8-20). Fasten the furring strips with concrete nails and space them 7 7/8 inches on centers (Fig. 8-21)—from the middle of one strip to the middle of the next one above. After the furring strips are in place, the installation is the same as described for a plasterboard surface.

When driving the concrete nails, do not use a nail hammer; use a short-handled sledge hammer of a 2-pound ball peen hammer. Nails used to fasten the shingles to the furring strips should be 3/4 inch long.

Finishing is a matter of taste. Many people use no finish at all. There is, however, a wide variety of transparent and opaque pigmented stains for almost any kind of finish you desire.

Fig. 8-19. Cove molding or other trim is applied over the last shingles to give a finished appearance.

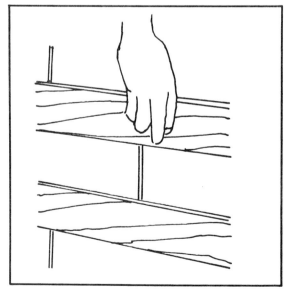

Fig. 8-20. On concrete or masonry, 4-inch-wide furring strips are fastened to the wall with concrete nails about every 12 inches.

160

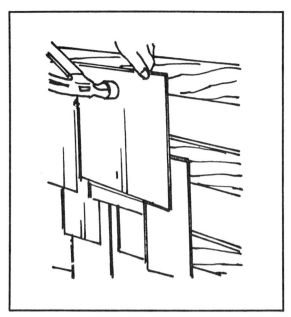

Fig. 8-21. Furring strips are spaced 7 7/8 inches on center. Panel strips are nailed to furring in overlapping courses to the top.

USE WOOD STRIPS FOR UNUSUAL WALL DECORATIONS

It's amazing what you can do in the way of wall decoration with a few strips of polished wood that reach from floor to ceiling. Those shown in Fig. 8-22 are made of mahogany and are stained a dark reddish brown color. They are finished with two coats of varnish, each rubbed down with steel wool and polished with a final coat of paste wax. They measure 8 feet × 1 1/2 inches × 1 1/2 inches and have 1/4-inch grooves running the length of each side.

They are fastened to the wall with 3-inch flathead brass screws driven flush with the surface. The screws go through the plasterboard and into the studs. Molly bolts or similar fasteners are used where studs are not available.

The use of full-length wall strips with an attractive furniture finish offers great flexibility in choice of decorative surfaces. The wall space between the strips can be painted or papered.

Fig. 8-22. Wood strips as wall decorations.

You can, however, use much more than paint and paper. Note how venetian blinds have been used between strips at the left in Fig. 8-22. Mirrors can also be used with startling effect, especially when two of them are used at right angles to each other in the corner.

Another interesting possibility is the use of prefinished murals, such as the flower design shown in a panel in Fig. 8-22. Several of the major wall paneling manufacturers make murals mounted on 1/4-inch hardboard with a clear waterproof finish. The murals, which come in a broad variety of designs, can be inserted into the 1/4-inch grooves of the strips (Fig. 8-23). Doing so will put the mural 3/4 inch forward from the wall and create a very interesting accent.

The strips do not have to be expensive hardwood. You can use any kind of softwood finished to your taste.

USE COMMON WOOD MOLDINGS TO CREATE PICTURE FRAMES

Framing paintings, prints, and photographs can be stimulating and fun when you use wood molding to make your own frames. The different kinds of moldings available from any building materials dealer along with the different finishes available give you an inexpensive way to mix and match frames in endless combinations for all your picture-framing needs. You can also find more elaborate moldings at a picture-framing specialty store, but they want to make the frame for you rather than just sell you the molding. Moreover, their moldings are much more expensive.

Making your own frames from moldings is easy and requires only a few basic tools that are found in most home workshops. These include a light hammer, nail set, corner fasteners, ruler, finishing nails with small heads, white glue, fine sandpaper,

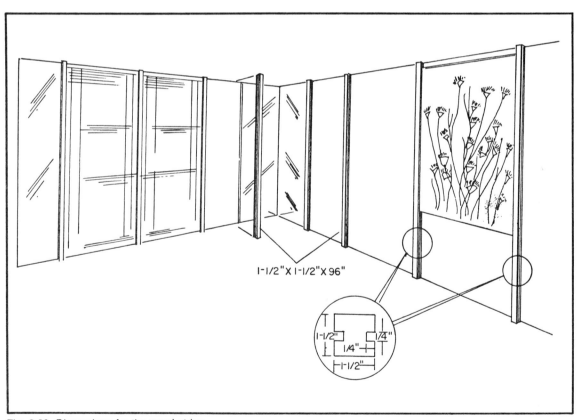

Fig. 8-23. Dimensions for the wood strips.

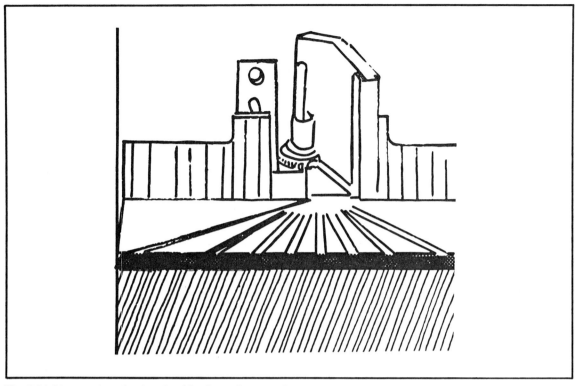

Fig. 8-24. You need a miter box for this picture frame project.

fine-toothed saw, and a pencil. You'll also need a miter box for making accurate 45-degree corner cuts (the miter box can be rented if you don't want to buy one) (Fig. 8-24) and a set of four miter corner clamps (Fig. 8-25). If you buy a miter box, make sure to buy a fine-toothed back saw to fit it. This is an inexpensive saw with 11 teeth to the inch and a steel reinforcement along the top edge. You don't have to spend much money on a miter box, either. You only need one as a guide for your backsaw, and there is one which looks like a wood trough or channel with a 45-degree and a 90-degree sawcut across it. This type only costs a few dollars. The miter clamps are also inexpensive and are available in most hardware stores.

Moldings that are designed as picture frames have a rabbet or step cut into them at the back, along the inner edge. When the moldings are put together in a four-sided frame, the step all around the inner edge forms a recess into which you can lay the glass, the mat, the picture, and backing on

which it is mounted. The inexpensive moldings available to you at lumber and building supply stores do not, however, have this rabbet or step; so you must provide your own.

To make a step, you simply glue or nail (or both) a strip of wood to the back of the molding you have chosen for the frame. The strip can be another piece of molding smaller than the main frame and of a suitable thickness to form a shelf to contain the picture and its backing, mat, and glass, if any. The mat referred to here is a piece of white cardboard with a square or rectangular hole that fits over the picture and forms a margin all around it. The edges of the opening are always beveled. Beveling cutters for this purpose can be bought in most art supply stores.

Various examples of different combinations of moldings you can use to make your picture frames are shown in Fig. 8-26—use them or create your own.

Wood molding is sold by the lineal foot and is

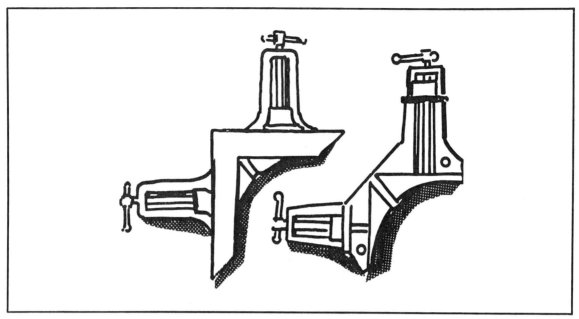

Fig. 8-25. You also need a set of four corner clamps.

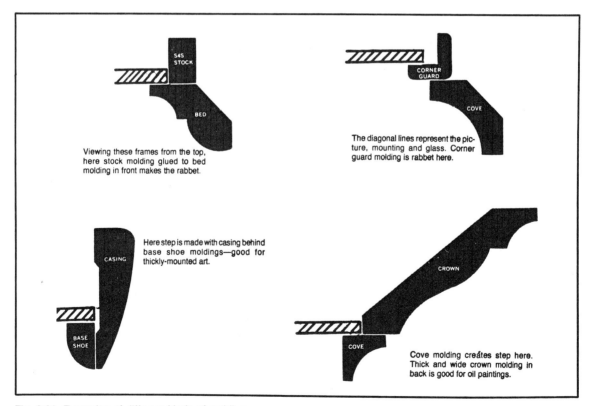

Viewing these frames from the top, here stock molding glued to bed molding in front makes the rabbet.

The diagonal lines represent the picture, mounting and glass. Corner guard molding is rabbet here.

Here step is made with casing behind base shoe moldings—good for thickly-mounted art.

Cove molding creates step here. Thick and wide crown molding in back is good for oil paintings.

Fig. 8-26. Examples of different kinds of moldings.

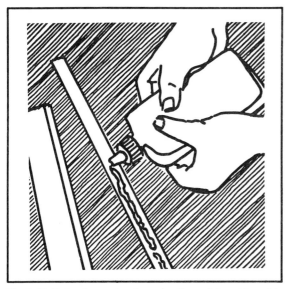

Fig. 8-27. To begin construction, glue the molding strips with white glue and clamp them until dry.

available in lengths from 3 to 16 feet. Buy the shorter lengths when possible because the grade requirements are higher for these lengths.

After you have determined the type of frame and mat that you want and have selected your moldings, you are ready to begin construction. Glue the smaller step molding to the larger frame molding so that they form one long strip (Fig. 8-27). Clamp or nail this strip until the glue has set, then cut off one end of your new molding strip at a 45-degree angle (Fig. 8-28).

Now measure the length of the bottom edge of the picture, add 1/8-inch to this measurement, and then transfer this measurement to the molding (Fig. 8-29). To do this start from the end already mitered and lay your ruler along the smaller molding that forms the picture rabbet or step as shown in Fig. 8-29. Mark and then cut a 45-degree miter at this measurement in the opposite angle of the one or

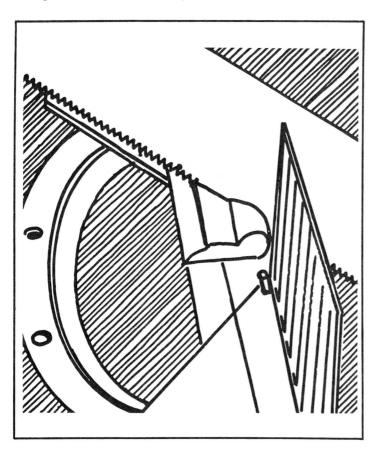

Fig. 8-28. Cut corners carefully at a 45-degree angle to ensure mitered corners. Use a miter box to be sure they are accurate.

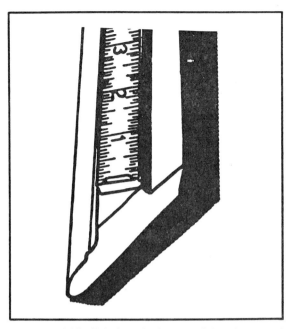

Fig. 8-29. Add 1/8 inch to the bottom of the picture and transfer this measurement to the molding along the picture rabbet made by the two moldings.

the other end. This is the bottom of the frame—you'll also need an identical strip at the top. Measure a second piece from the first and cut.

Now measure the side edge of your picture and cut two pieces of molding for the sides the same way as for the top and bottom. Be sure to remember to add the extra 1/8 inch before cutting the first side piece.

Now that you have the four sides, you can begin to assemble the picture frame. Take one side piece and the bottom piece, coat the ends to be joined with white glue, and then place them carefully in one of the corner clamps (Fig. 8-30). Align the corner perfectly and then tighten the clamp just enough so that the pieces will hold together rigidly when you nail the corner together (Fig. 8-31).

Drive two or more of the finishing nails through the corner from each side most of the way in, allowing the heads to protrude about 1/16 to 1/8 inch to avoid denting the picture frame (Fig. 8-32). Then carefully finish driving the nails with a small nail set so that the heads are about 1/16 inch below the

Fig. 8-30. After you have cut a side piece of the frame, apply white glue to both mitered surfaces that are to be joined.

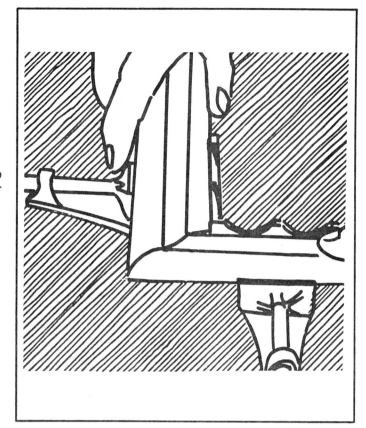

Fig. 8-31. Clamp the corner made by the two mitered and glued surfaces tightly with a miter clamp and wipe off the excess glue.

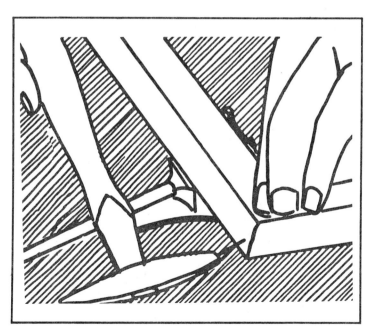

Fig. 8-32. Drive a small-headed finishing nail into each edge of the clamped corner. Allow the heads to protrude 1/16 to 1/8 inch.

surface of the molding (Fig. 8-33).

Fill the nail hole with a little wood putty or fine sawdust mixed with white glue (you can use the sawdust obtained while cutting the frame) and let dry. If the molding you chose is fairly wide, use a corrugated fastener to further strengthen the joint. Using the other three corner clamps, follow this same procedure on the other three corners and allow the glue to dry thoroughly. If you only have one or two corner clamps, you can still build the frame, but it will take a little longer because you have to let each corner dry thoroughly together in the clamp before going on to the next one. When the glue is dry, sand the frame lightly with fine sandpaper (Fig. 8-34).

There are many ways that you can finish your picture frame: again your choice depends upon the picture and the type of effect you wish to obtain. You can use paste wax, varnish, lacquer, shellac, stain, antique glaze and texture, or paint. You can

also buy prefinished wood molding, if you don't want to finish it yourself.

A good natural finish is two or three coats of white shellac (with a light sanding or smoothing with fine steel wool after each coat) followed by a buffing with a good grade of paste wax. This same shellac and wax treatment can also be applied over a coat of a desired stain after it has dried.

Glazing and texturing with paint are more time-consuming methods of finishing the frame, but they're more expressive, too, allowing you to match the frame to the tone and texture of the picture. Brush on a coat of gray, heavy-bodied latex paint and before it dries, texture the surfaces that you wish to treat. Lining with steel wool, a comb, or stippling with a cellulose sponge are a few of the many textures you can create.

BUILD YOUR OWN CLOSET

If you build a closet in an internal corner of a room,

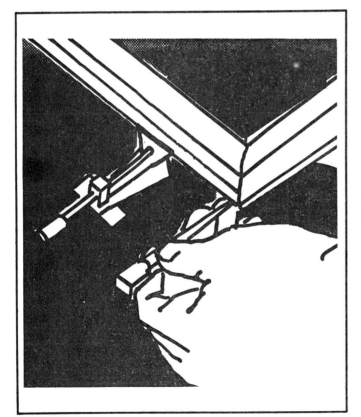

Fig. 8-33. Use a nail set to set these protruding nail heads about 1/16 inch below the surface of the frame to prevent denting.

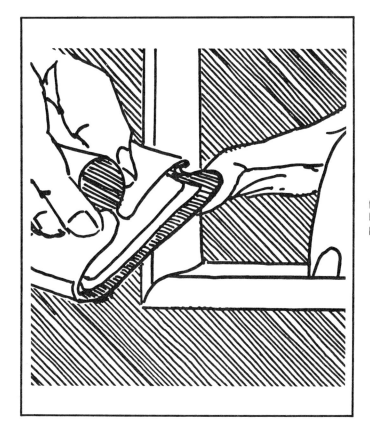

Fig. 8-34. After the glue has set and the frame has been built, sand it lightly with fine sandpaper, going with the grain.

you can save a considerable amount of time in framing and finishing. You can use the two existing walls as closet walls. Inasmuch as the door, door jamb, and header will take up almost all of the third wall, you need only stud out one side wall, long enough to fit your closet depth requirements.

The most important dimension of the project is the door width. If you choose a 2-foot-×-6-foot-8-inch door—a popular size assuming 8-foot ceilings—the minimum width of the door wall must be 3 feet to provide room for the structural studding and inside door casing, as shown in Fig. 8-35. You can, of course, make the door wall wider than the minimum simply by adding more studding.

Starting the Job

Once you've chosen the door width, calculate the width of the door wall as explained in Fig. 8-36, and decide the width of the side wall (closet depth). Lay

out these dimensions on the floor, making all corners square with the aid of a rafter square. Remove the base molding from that area of the wall, and you're ready to begin the work.

Cut all plates and the studs that fit between them to size (Table 8-1). Note that the top plates are lapped at the external corner at the top of the corner pier (point X in Fig. 8-35). Facenail the sole plates to the floor with 16d common nails. Toenail the stud to both sole and top plates, as well as the corner pier to the floor, with four 10d common nails at each attachment point (Fig. 8-37).

Cut the header, shown in Fig. 8-38, to a length of the rough opening width plus 3 inches. The width of the rough opening dimension is the door width plus 2 1/2 inches, and the height is the door height plus 2 inches.

Next assemble and toenail the header into the structure as shown, with the trimmers supporting its weight. Although you could get away without

169

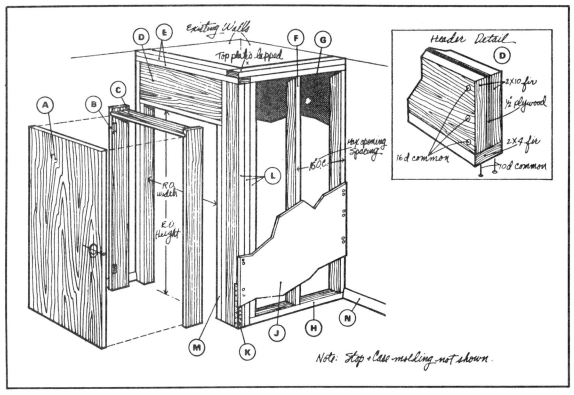

Fig. 8-35. An exploded view of the closet.

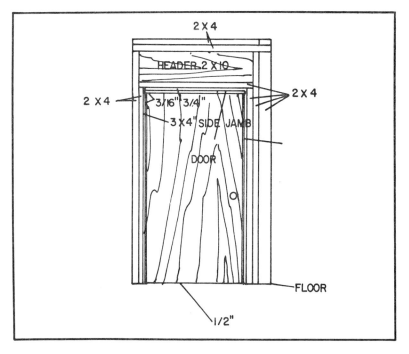

Fig. 8-36. Door Wall Dimensions.

170

Table 8-1. Materials for the Closet.

A. 1 3/8"-1 3/4" door, 2'0" × 6'8"
B. side jamb
C. head jamb
D. header (see detail)
E. top plates 2" × 4" fir
F. stud 2" × 4" fir
G. inside sheetrock 1/2"
H. sole plate 2" × 4" fir
J. outside sheetrock 1/2"
K. metal corner bead
L. built-up corner pier 2" × 4" fir
M. trimmer
N. base molding

Fig. 8-38. The header is toenailed into the studding. The top plates in the corner and trimmer studs support the header weight.

using a solid header, it is standard practice to use one in so many other types of projects that it's worth the slight extra cost to get the practice on this job. Now, make a final check of the rough opening dimensions before you proceed.

Installing the Drywall

The average closet can be enclosed with two 4-×-8 pieces of 1/2-inch sheetrock applied horizontally. It's best to start on the inside to take advantage of the available light. Score, fold, and cut off the sheetrock pieces with a razor knife, as shown in Fig. 8-39. Drive in the 1 1/2-inch sheetrock nails about 6 inches apart, leaving a slightly dimpled impres-

sion of the hammer face at each nail head to receive joint compound later.

Install the outside sheetrock, and trim all exposed edges with a surfoam plane. Nail on the corner bead, using enough nails to flatten any bulges in the bead flanges (Fig. 8-40).

Apply tape and jointing compound to all internal corners and butt joints, following the instructions on the packaging. It's best to apply the compound in several thin layers, sanding in between when dry. Use increasingly wider-bladed jointing knives on each subsequent layer to get the professional "feathered" effect (Fig. 8-41).

Now fill in all nail-head dimples and the corner-

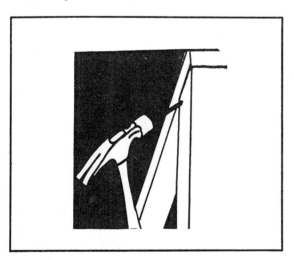

Fig. 8-37. Built-up corner pier of the closet frame is toenailed to the top plates with 10d common nails.

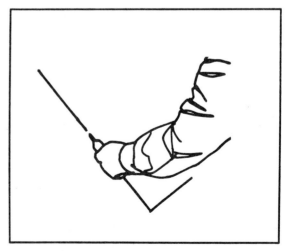

Fig. 8-39. Sheetrock is scored then folded to crack. The cut is completed with a knife on the second side.

Fig. 8-40. All exposed sheetrock edges on the closet walls are then smoothed with a surface plane.

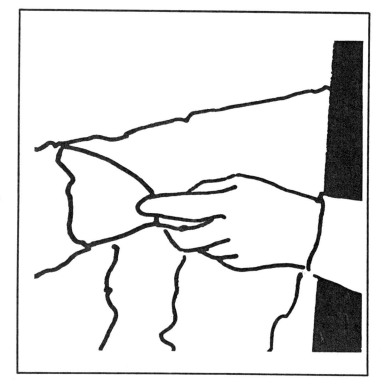

Fig. 8-41. Compound goes over the joint, then tape is applied, followed by more compound.

bead area with joint compound, applied in several layers as before. Sanding with silicon carbide "fastcut" 100-grit paper gets the job done in a hurry.

Fitting the Door Jamb

The jamb set comes from the lumberyard or home center as a three-piece group (two sides and a head), all oversized. First, trim down the head (see Fig. 8-35 inset for calculation) to fix the distance between the side jambs, allowing the proper door-to-jamb clearance (Fig. 8-42). It must be held constant from top to bottom.

Now check the calculation in the inset of Fig. 8-35 and trim one side jamb to this height. Tack this jamb against one side of the rough opening with

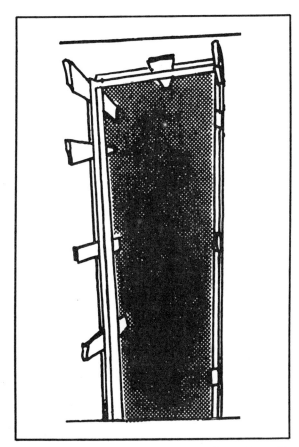

Fig. 8-42. The jamb in the rough opening is trued up with shakes for the right door-to-jamb clearance.

the lower end of the side jamb resting on the floor. Place a level across the rough opening and mark the place on the opposite side which corresponds to the top of the first side jamb to ensure a level head jamb. Take the second side jamb and trim the bottom, if necessary, to fit the mark you just made on the second side of the rough opening.

Identify the side jambs and then assemble them to the head jamb on the floor with 10d rosin-coated box nails. Place the trimmed jamb assembly back into the rough opening according to your marks, and start to insert pairs of tapered undercourse shakes into the gap between one of the side jambs and its rough opening trimmer stud (one shake from the inside of the closet and one from the outside as shown). This process will move the side jamb away slightly from the trimmer stud, while the tapered shakes keep the jamb parallel to the trimmer. Pushing both shakes together increases the gap width; pulling them apart decreases the gap.

The idea is to get this jamb dead plumb and dead straight; so take your time here. This is another one of those spots where you want the professional look. Start by creating about a 3/8-inch gap and continue up and down the jamb, checking with at least a 4-foot level before you drive in the 10d finishing nails to lock jamb, tapers, and trimmer. Make sure you put tapers behind all future hinge and striker locations for structural rigidity.

Note: Be sure to drive the nails in about 1/2 inch further back on the jamb then the thickness of the door you are using so they'll be covered up by the door stop molding you will install later.

Now insert the door temporarily and check the straightness of the first jamb side and, if necessary, make adjustments. Repeat the wedge operation on the second jamb side and check again with the door. After wedging the head jamb with shakes as before, make a final check with the door for uniform clearance (a total on both sides of 3/16 inch). Cut off all shakes flush at the jambs with a razor knife.

Hanging the Door

Mark the outlines of the door hinges on the edge of the door between 7 1/2 and 11 inches from both top and bottom ends, using a 3 1/2-×-3 1/2 butt hinge as a template. Make stop cuts around the outline with a chisel, as shown in Fig. 8-43, and then gradually chisel out the waste wood, making the hinge mortises. Keep checking the depth with the hinge until the hinge fits flush in the mortise.

Set the door into the jamb and block it up to the proper height from the floor, and even with the side jambs, using scrap undercourse shakes. Transfer the locations of the tops and bottoms of both hinges from the door to the jamb, as Fig. 8-44 shows. Now use a try square to extend these four marks back horizontally onto the jamb. Mark the exact hinge position on the jamb to allow the door to fit flush. Repeat the hinge mortising procedure on the jamb and install the door hinges and door temporarily for a final check of fit (Fig. 8-45).

Installing the Lock

Dismount the door, lay it down flat, and use the template provided with the cylindrical lock hard-

ware to locate the centers of the lock body and latch holes, as shown in Fig. 8-46 (a Schlage key type was used here). The backset is automatically controlled by the folded template so you need only place the template centerline 40 inches from the top or bottom end of the door.

Drill out both holes, chisel out the latch plate mortise as shown in Fig. 8-47, and install the lock. Remount the door, then locate, drill out, and chisel the striker plate mortise and install the striker (Fig. 8-48).

Finishing Up

Install the door stop with 6d finishing nails and set them in for putty. Make sure the stop is flush against the closed, latched door. Install the casing with mitered corners, as shown in Fig. 8-49, with 6d finishing nails.

Step back and admire your work before you begin painting or staining. There are prehung doors

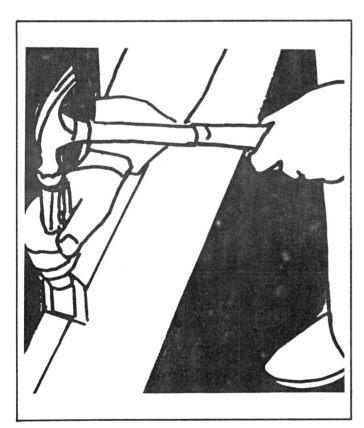

Fig. 8-43. To install the hinges, first make stop cuts with a butt chisel around the hinge outline on the door edge.

174

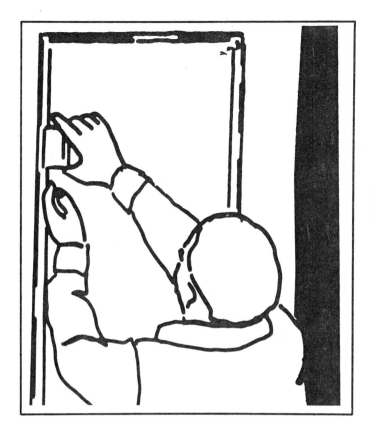

Fig. 8-44. Wedge the door into the jamb with undercourse shakes. Carry the hinge marks form the door to the jamb edge.

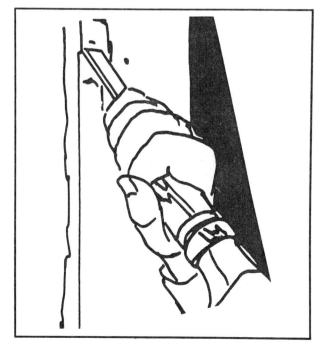

Fig. 8-45. Mortise the jamb. The jamb nail to the right of the chisel top will be hidden by the door stop.

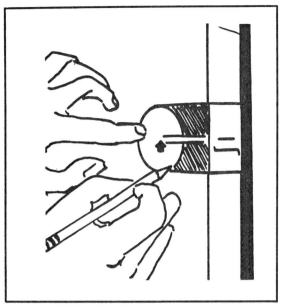

Fig. 8-46. Hold or tape a template at the door edge and make marks to drill the lock and latch holes.

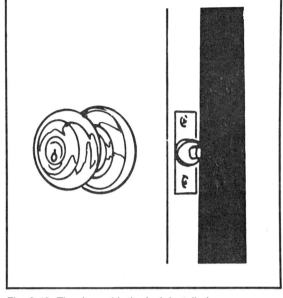

Fig. 8-48. The door with the lock installed.

available with the jambs assembled (but not trimmed), lock holes bored, and hinges mortised and mounted. While they save time, however, they do add to the cost.

PANEL YOUR CLOSETS WITH CEDAR

Remember the good smell of cedar when you opened Grandma's attic closet or that old bedroom chest where she hid quilts and extra blankets? Now

Fig. 8-47. Make a mortise for the latch plate in the door edge after scribing the outline of the latch plate.

Fig. 8-49. After you hang the door, miter cornered side casing is installed on the outside of the door jamb.

Fig. 8-50. A closet paneled with cedar.

with a new type of closet panel, you can line your closets with red cedar at minimum cost and effort (Fig. 8-50).

Called Cedarline, the panels are made from thin flakes of Tennessee Aromatic Red Cedar and fully retain the moth-repelling aroma of the natural wood. They come in standard 4-×-8-foot and 16-×-48-inch panels, 1/4 inch thick, sanded on one side. Either side may be used, but the unsanded surface of compressed flakes gives an unusual and beautiful effect.

The panels are easy to install. First, measure the walls and any other surfaces in your closets you wish to line with cedar panels (Fig. 8-51). It will save both time and material to outline how the panels are to be installed before you cut them. Plan to have the edges of the panels centered over a wall stud where joints are necessary.

Remove shelves, molding, light fixtures, and any other items as necessary. Cut the panels as required to fit. Either a power saw or hand saw may be used (Fig. 8-52). Use 1 1/4-inch finishing nails to fasten the panels, driving them through the existing wall material into the studs. These panels won't split, and you'll discover the finishing nail

Fig. 8-51. Accurate measurement of the closet will save waste when you cut the panels.

Fig. 8-52. A power saw works well to cut the panels. A hand saw will also produce good results.

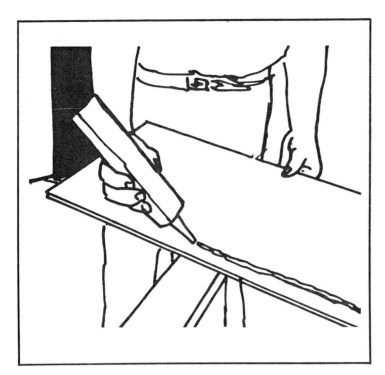

Fig. 8-53. Use regular panel adhesive or finishing nails to mount the panels.

heads are virtually impossible to detect against the flake background. You may use regular panel adhesive instead of finishing nails to mount the panels on wall, floor, and ceiling surfaces (Fig. 8-53). If you have trouble finding the studs, adhesives will do the job as well as nails.

Start the panels on the back wall, where visibility is most important (Fig. 8-54). If you use a panel adhesive, it will hold without the need of undue pressure. The panels will fit together snugly. The joint is virtually imperceptible as a result of the random-flake overall pattern of the cedar panels.

The floor should also be covered with panels (Fig. 8-55). This gives the closet a cedar-closet effect with the scent of cedar surrounding the clothes, and therefore, gives more complete mothproof protection to the clothing.

When you have the closet completely paneled, stop a moment and study your closet carefully. You may find many ways to increase its usefulness by using racks and shelves in otherwise wasted space. Use any leftover pieces of the paneling to cover the shelves.

Fig. 8-54. The panels should be mounted on the back of the wall first since it is the most visible area.

178

Fig. 8-55. The floor should be covered with panels too. Then the cedar scent surrounds the clothes.

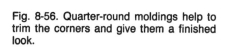

Fig. 8-56. Quarter-round moldings help to trim the corners and give them a finished look.

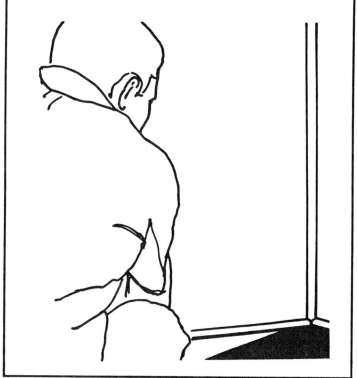

After you have placed shelves and closet rods to your satisfaction, give your job a professional appearance with 3/4-inch quarter-round corner molding, taking care to miter the joints (Fig. 8-56). Reinstall the original baseboard and molding if you desire, remembering to trim it slightly to take care of the smaller closet dimensions. If you would like to install new baseboard or shelves, remember that cedar is particularly attractive and blends well with the cedar panels, but many suitable combinations with other woods are also possible to suite your individual taste.

Do not apply paint or any other sealers to the panels, or you'll seal in the cedar aroma. Keep your closet tightly closed, and you will have a mothproof aromatic closet for years to come.

Appendix

Appendix

WOOD

Hardwoods and softwoods are classified botanically as broad-leaved and needle-bearing trees respectively. This classification is misleading, however. For example, basswood, which is classified as a hardwood, is actually softer than yellow pine, which is classified as a softwood.

The following list gives the color and uses of various hardwoods.

Hardwoods

Apple. Pinkish-brown in color, apple wood is a strong, hard, tough wood. It is generally available in small pieces only. Traditionally apple wood has been used for tool handles.

Ash. Black ash is a dark grayish-brown wood. Oregon and white ash are grayish-brown, but they sometimes have a reddish tinge.

Balsa. Balsa is a very lightweight wood, and it is not very strong. It is used to a great extent in building model airplanes.

Basswood. Basswood is creamy white to creamy brown in color, with an occasional reddish tinge. Generally uniform in color with little distinguishable grain, basswood is an excellent wood for carving and sculpturing.

Beech. Beech is white with a reddish to a reddish-brown tinge. When quartersawed, the rays appear as small, dark brown flecks. Beech is apt to be unstable, but it is an excellent wood to use when the part calls for steam bending.

Birch. Birch is an excellent wood for toy construction and is readily available. The color varies from a light brown to a dark reddish-brown. It is heavy, hard, and dense.

Boxwood. Boxwood, a fine-textured wood, yellow in color, is extremely heavy. It is an excellent wood for turning and carving, but it is generally available in small pieces only.

Brazilwood. Brazilwood is a dark red wood of fine texture. It is quite hard and heavy, although it can be worked fairly easily with sharp tools. Originally this wood was highly valued as a source of red dye.

Bubinga. Bubinga is a reddish-brown hardwood from West Africa.

Butternut. Butternut, sometimes called white walnut, can be used as a substitute for black walnut for toy construction, but it does not have the hardness, strength, and beauty of black walnut.

Cherry. Cherry, a rather heavy, dense, close-grained wood, varies in color from light red to dark reddish-brown. Sometimes it is known as wild cherry, black cherry, or choke cherry.

Chestnut. The heartwood of chestnut is grayish-brown or brown and becomes darker as it ages. Clear chestnut is hard to find today. Most available chestnut today is "wormy chestnut" and is used mostly for paneling.

Cottonwood. Cottonwood or poplar, a grayish-white to light-brown wood, can be used in place of basswood or white pine.

Cocobolo. Cocobolo is a heavy, dense wood that is basically orange-red, but streaked with darker stripes.

Ebony. A very heavy, hardwood, ebony is generally a dense black, but it may be a medium to dark brown according to species. It tends to be very brittle and must be worked with considerable care.

Elm. There are six species of elm grown in the United States: American elm, slippery elm, rock elm, winged elm, cedar elm, and September elm. The heartwood is generally a light brown with traces of red. Elm can be steam bent with ease.

Hickory. Hickory varies from white, in its sapwood, to a reddish color, in its heartwood. It is a very tough, heavy, hard, strong, flexible wood, and it is an excellent wood for parts that are small in cross section.

Holly. See Boxwood.

Magnolia. Magnolia is a straight-grained wood of close, uniform texture. The sapwood varies from yellowish-white to dark brown tinted with yellow or green. It is similar in characteristics to yellow poplar.

Mahogany. Mahogany, a stable wood, is generally a pink to reddish-brown in color, is fairly easy to fashion, and takes an excellent finish. There are many species, including African, American, Cuban, and Philippine.

Maple. Maple and birch are probably the two best light-colored hardwoods for toy construction. Maple is a creamy white and will remain so with age. It is quite readily available.

Oak. The two large categories of oak are red oak and white oak. Red oak is probably better to use in toy construction because of its color and highly conspicuous broad rays when the lumber is quarter-sawed.

Padauk. Padauk in most species is a brilliant red, and in that respect resembles Brazilwood. This beautiful wood is ideal for color accents on toys. Considering its weight and hardness, it is not a difficult wood to fashion with standard woodworking tools.

Pear. Pear wood is strong, heavy, and tough. It is very stable when dry and for that reason is many times used in making drawing instruments and rulers. It is also a fine wood for carving and making toys. The color is a pinkish-brown.

Poplar. See Cottonwood.

Purple Wood. This distinct wood, as you would assume, is purple and comes from Dutch Guiana. It is tough, dense, and strong. If you possess carbide-tipped tools, you should consider purple, wood, but the wood would dull the edges of standard cutters very rapidly.

Rosewood. Rosewood from South America is reddish-brown with dark streaks running through it. Rosewood from the East Indies is a deep red or purple. It is very heavy and extremely hard; so it is difficult to work with it.

Sassafras. Sassafras, a wood at one time used by Indians to make dugout canoes, is a moderately heavy wood often confused with black ash. The heartwood varies from a dull grayish-brown to a dark brown. It does not have a high priority as a toymaking material.

Sweet Gum. Sweet gum, often used as a substitute for walnut in furniture construction, has a reddish-brown heartwood.

Satinwood. Satinwood, often used for inlays and furniture parts, comes from Ceylon and is light yellow in color.

Sycamore. Sycamore is a fine-textured wood, and is reddish-brown in color. Figured sycamore is highly prized as a wood for use on the backs of violins, and for that reason is sometimes called "fiddle back sycamore."

Teak. Teak is almost a universal wood. It varies from light brown to dark brown and comes from Thailand and Burma. It is a very heavy wood and will sink in water when it is green. It is difficult to use because of its abrasive nature. It is used extensively for shipbuilding and furniture construction. You should have considerable patience when working with this wood.

Walnut. American black walnut has long been cherished as a furniture and architectural wood. This beautiful, rich dark brown wood is strong, hard, and heavy but works well with the standard woodworking tools.

Zebrawood. A distinctive wood from Western Africa, zebrawood is identified by alternate stripes of light tan and dark brown or black, and it gets its name from this feature.

Softwoods

Cedar. There are many kinds of cedar: Alaska, incense, Eastern red, Southern red, Western red, and white.

Eastern and Southern cedar are the best woods for toys. These woods are used extensively for making pencils, novelties, small boats, scientific instruments, and chests.

Douglas Fir. Douglas fir, grown in the western part of the United States, varies widely in weight and strength. Whenever a wood is needed with contrast between spring and summer growth, you might try Douglas fir.

Hemlock. Western hemlock has limited use as a toy material, but it can be used in "sandwich" construction when protected by harder lumber. This wood often contains small, black knots that do not necessarily detract from its use.

Redwood. Redwood from the large sequoia varies from a light brown to a dark mahogany color. It is easy to work with straight-grained wood. Its pleasing color is suitable for toy parts with large cross sections. It is particularly valuable as a material for making outdoor toys because of its durability and resistance to decay.

White Pine. Eastern white pine and sugar pine are the best selections for toy construction, because of their straight-grained, uniform texture. This wood has a creamy-pinkish color which turns a light orange-red with age. It is readily available and is easy to work with ordinary woodworking tools.

Glossary

Glossary

annular rings—The concentric rings in the cross-section of a tree that form the grain pattern; one ring is added each year.

apron—A piece of wood in the form of a rail, usually below a drawer.

backboard—The wood forming the back of a cabinet or block of shelves.

bail—A swinging loop handle.

batten—Any narrow strip of wood. It may be across other boards to join them, cover a gap, or prevent warping. It may support a shelf.

blind—Not right through, such as a stopped hole or mortise.

bracket—An angular piece used to support a shelf or flap.

cabinet—Any case or boxlike structure, usually with shelves, drawers, and doors.

cabinetmaking, cabinetry—The craft of making all kinds of furniture; not just cabinets.

cast—Twisting of a surface that should be flat.

chamfer—An angle or bevel planed on an edge.

clamp—A device for drawing things, especially joints, together. The tool may be called a cramp. Wood used as a clamp may be called a cleat.

closet—A cupboard for storing clothes and other things. A small room.

core—Base wood on which veneer is laid.

counterbore—To drill a large hole over a small one so the screw head in it is drawn below the surface and can be covered by a plug.

countersink—To bevel the top of a hole so a flat-headed screw can be driven level with the surface.

cupboard—A closet or cabinet particularly intended for storing cups, saucers, plates, and food.

dado—A groove cut across the grain, usually to support the end of a shelf.

dovetail—The fan-shaped piece that projects between pins in the other part of a dovetail joint.

dowel—A cylindrical piece of wood used as a peg when making joints.

escutcheon—A keyhole or the plate covering and surrounding it. A shield bearing a coat-of-arms.

fall front—A flap that lets down to be supported in a horizontal position.

fastenings (fasteners)—Collective name for anything used for joining, such as nails and screws.

featheredge—A wide, smooth bevel, taking the edge

of a board to a very thin line.

fillet—A strip of wood used between parts to join or support them.

fillister—A rabbet plane with fences to control the depth and width of cut.

framed construction—Furniture or other woodwork where the main parts are formed of wood strips around panels.

gauge—A marking tool or a means of testing.

half-lap joint—Two crossing pieces notched into each other, usually to bring their surfaces level.

handed—Made as a pair.

hanging stile—The upright at the side of a door to which the hinges are attached.

haunch—A short cutback part of a tenon that joins another piece near its end.

housing joint—Another name for a dado joint, particularly where a shelf is supported in a groove in another piece of wood.

jointing—The making of any joint, but particularly planing edges straight to make close glued joints, edge-to-edge.

kerf—The slot formed by the cut of a saw.

laminate—To construct in layers with several pieces of wood glued together, particularly in the making of curved parts. Plywood is made by laminating veneers.

lap joint—The general name for joints where one piece of wood is cut to overlap and fit into another.

lineal—Length only. The term is sometimes used when pricing wood.

locking stile—The upright against which a door shuts.

matched boarding—Joining boards edge to edge with matching tongues and grooves, or less commonly with the edges rabbeted to lap over each other.

miter—A joint where the meeting angle of the surfaces is divided or bisected, as in the corner of a picture frame or plinth.

mortise-and-tenon joint—A method of joining the end of one piece of wood into the side of another, with the tenon projecting like a tongue on the end of one piece to fit into the matching mortise cut in the other piece.

nosing—A semicircular molding.

pedestal—A supporting post.

pegging—Putting dowels or wooden pegs through joints.

piercing—A decoration made by cutting through the wood.

pigeon hole—A storage compartment built into a writing desk.

pilot hole—A small hole drilled as a guide for the drill point before making a larger hole.

planted—Applied instead of cut in the solid. Molding attached to a surface is planted. If it is cut in the solid wood, it is stuck.

plinth—The base part around the bottom of a piece of furniture.

plowed (ploughed)—Grooved along the grain, usually to take a panel.

plywood—A board made with veneers glued in laminations with the grain of each layer square to the next.

rabbet—An angular cutout section at an edge, as in the back of a picture frame.

rail—A member in framing, usually horizontal.

rake—Inclined to the horizontal.

rod—A strip of wood with distances of construction details marked on it, to use for comparing parts, instead of measuring with a rule.

router—A power or hand tool for leveling the bottom of a groove or recessed surface. With special cutters it can cut moldings and other shapes.

rule—A measuring rod.

run—In a long length. Lumber quantity can be quoted as so many feet run.

setting out—Laying out details, usually full-size, of a piece of furniture or other construction.

shelf—A flat board fixed horizontally on which to store things.

slat—A narrow, thin wood.

splay—Spread out.

spline—A narrow strip of wood fitting into grooves, usually to strengthen two meeting surfaces that are to be glued.

stile—A vertical member in door framing.

strap hinge—A hinge with long, narrow arms.

stretcher—A lengthwise rail between the lower parts of a table or similar assembly.

stub tenon (stopped tenon)—One that does not go through the other piece of wood. It fits into a blind mortise.

template—A shaped pattern to draw around when marking out parts, usually when several must match.

trunnel (treenail)—A peg or dowel driven through a joint.

veneer—A very thin piece of wood intended to be glued to a backing, which could be wood or particleboard.

veneer pin—A very fine nail with a small head.

waney edge—The edge of a board that still has bark on it or is still showing the pattern of the outside of the tree.

winding—A board or assembly that is not flat and whose twist can be seen when sighting for one end.

Index

Index

Edited by Suzanne L. Cheatle